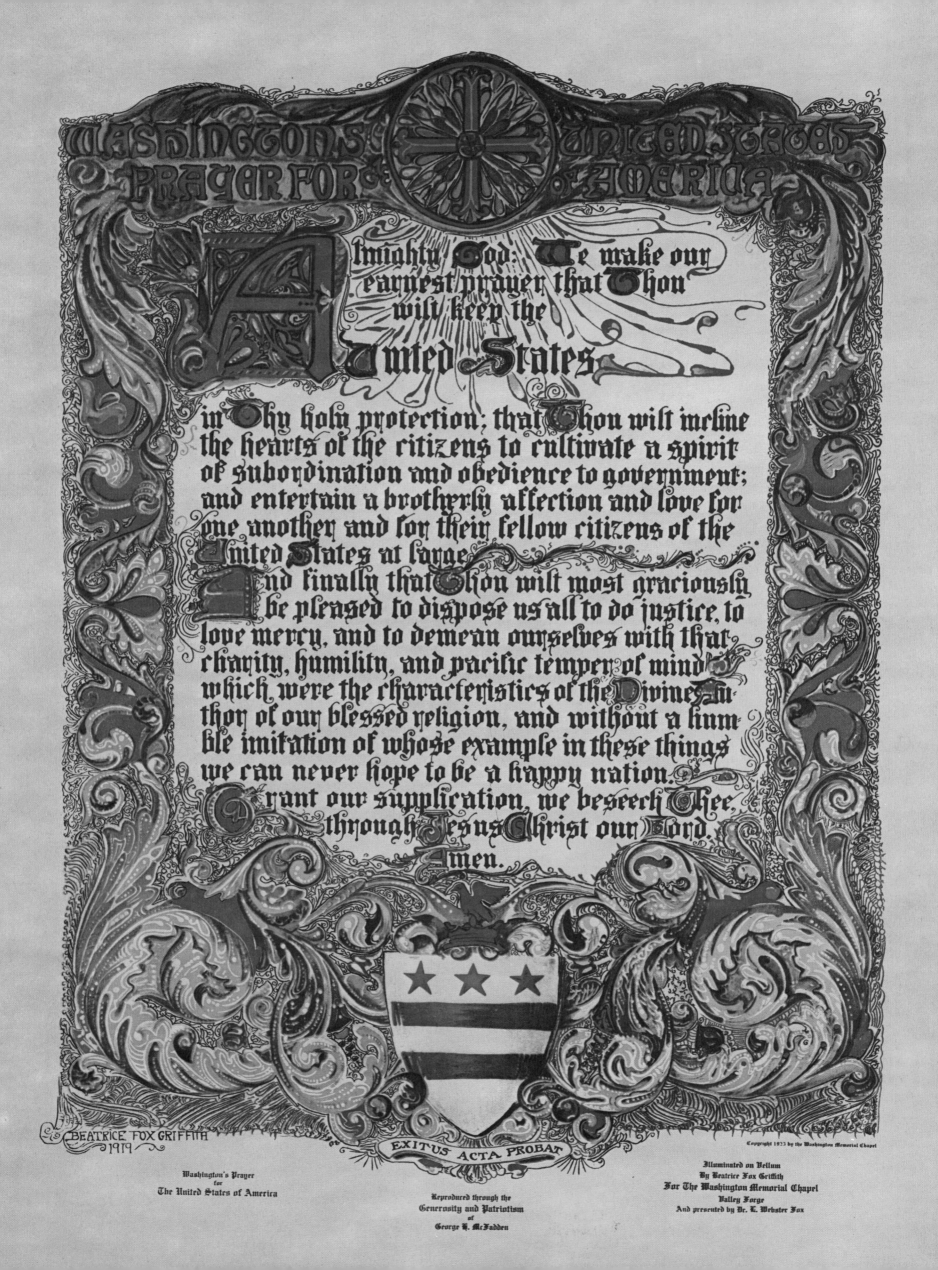

WASHINGTON'S PRAYER FOR UNITED STATES OF AMERICA

Almighty God: We make our earnest prayer that Thou wilt keep the United States in Thy holy protection; that Thou wilt incline the hearts of the citizens to cultivate a spirit of subordination and obedience to government; and entertain a brotherly affection and love for one another and for their fellow citizens of the United States at large.

And finally that Thou wilt most graciously be pleased to dispose us all to do justice, to love mercy, and to demean ourselves with that charity, humility, and pacific temper of mind which were the characteristics of the Divine Author of our blessed religion, and without a humble imitation of whose example in these things we can never hope to be a happy nation. Grant our supplication, we beseech Thee, through Jesus Christ our Lord. Amen.

BEATRICE FOX GRIFFITH 1919

EXITUS ACTA PROBAT

Copyright 1925 by the Washington Memorial Chapel

Washington's Prayer
for
The United States of America

Reproduced through the
Generosity and Patriotism
of
George H. McFadden

Illuminated on Vellum
By Beatrice Fox Griffith
For The Washington Memorial Chapel
Valley Forge
And presented by Dr. L. Webster Fox

VOLUME
FORTY-
FIVE

Christmas

AN AMERICAN ANNUAL OF CHRISTMAS LITERATURE AND ART

EDITED BY RANDOLPH E. HAUGAN

AUGSBURG PUBLISHING HOUSE • PUBLISHERS

MINNEAPOLIS

Table of Contents

Volume Forty-five

First Edition

Nineteen Hundred Seventy-five

The Christmas Gospel

Christmas Articles and Stories

Christmas Poetry

Christmas Music

Christmas Art

Christmas Illustrators

Melva Mickelson   *Edmund Kopietz*   *Audrey Teeple*

Acknowledgments

COVER: "WASHINGTON IN PRAYER AT VALLEY FORGE"
Rose window in the Valley Forge Memorial Bell Tower. Design by David Bramnick, executed by D'Ascenzo Studios, Merion Station, Pa.

FRONTISPIECE: "WASHINGTON'S PRAYER FOR THE UNITED STATES
        OF AMERICA" 2
Courtesy of Washington Memorial Chapel, Valley Forge, Pa.

MEMORIAL AT VALLEY FORGE 14–19
Illustration by Walter Swanson, page 14. Photos by Ronald E. Heaton, pages 15, 16 (bottom); Robert Narod, pages 16 (top), 18, 19; Wyco Colour Reproductions, page 17.

A DECLARATION OF INTERDEPENDENCE 20–26
Illustrations by William Medcalf. Calligraphy by Hildegard Szendrey.

A WALK THROUGH TIME 27–32
Photos courtesy of The Colonial Williamsburg Foundation, Williamsburg, Virginia. Photos, pages 27, 32, from *Christmas in Williamsburg*, published by the Colonial Williamsburg Foundation and distributed by Holt, Rinehart and Winston.

CHRISTMAS MUSIC 53–60
Calligraphy by Hildegard Szendrey.

A MORAVIAN CHRISTMAS 61–64
Photos courtesy of Old Salem, Inc., Winston-Salem, N.C.

BACK COVER: "VALLEY FORGE PARK"
Photo by Ronald E. Heaton.

LAYOUT AND DESIGN: GEORGE NORDWALL

MUSIC EDITOR: RUTH OLSON

According to St. Luke and St. Matthew

Illustrations by John Steel

AND IT CAME TO PASS in those days, that there went out a decree from Caesar Augustus, that all the world should be taxed (And this taxing was first made when Cyrenius was governor of Syria.) And all went to be taxed, every one into his own city. And Joseph also went up from Galilee, out of the city of Nazareth, into Judaea, unto the city of David, which is called Bethlehem; (because he was of the house and lineage of David:) To be taxed with Mary his espoused wife, being great with child. And so it was, that, while they were there, the days were accomplished that she should be delivered. And she brought forth her firstborn son, and wrapped him in swaddling clothes, and laid him in a manger; because there was no room for them in the inn. And there were in the same country shepherds abiding in the field, keeping watch over their flock by night. And, lo, the angel of the Lord came upon them, and the glory of the Lord shone round about them: and they were sore afraid.

AND THE ANGEL SAID unto them, Fear not: for behold, I bring you good tidings of great joy, which shall be to all people. For unto you is born this day in the city of David a Saviour, which is Christ the Lord. And this shall be a sign unto you; Ye shall find the babe wrapped in swaddling clothes, lying in a manger. And suddenly there was with the angel a multitude of the heavenly host praising God, and saying, Glory to God in the highest, and on earth peace, good will toward men. And it came to pass, as the angels were gone away from them into heaven, the shepherds said one to another, Let us now go even unto Bethlehem, and see this thing which is come to pass, which the Lord hath made known unto us. And they came with haste, and found Mary, and Joseph, and the babe lying in a manger. And when they had seen it, they made known abroad the saying which was told them concerning this child. And all they that heard it wondered at those things which were told them by the shepherds. But Mary kept all these things, and pondered them in her heart. And the shepherds returned, glorifying and praising God for all the things that they had heard and seen, as it was told unto them.

OW WHEN JESUS WAS born in Bethlehem of Judaea in the days of Herod the king, behold, there came wise men from the east to Jerusalem, Saying, Where is he that is born King of the Jews? for we have seen his star in the east, and are come to worship him. When Herod the king and heard these things, he was troubled, and all Jerusalem with him. And when he had gathered all the chief priests and scribes of the people together, he demanded of them where Christ should be born. And they said unto him, In Bethlehem of Judaea: for thus it is written by the prophet, And thou Bethlehem, in the land of Juda, art not the least among the princes of Juda: for out of thee shall come a Governor, that shall rule my people Israel. Then Herod, when he had privily called the wise men, enquired of them diligently what time the star appeared. And he sent them to Bethlehem, and said, Go and search diligently for the young child; and when ye have found him, bring me word again, that I may come and worship him also. When they had heard the king, they departed; and, lo, the star, which they saw in the east, went before them, till it came and stood over where the young child was. When they saw the star, they rejoiced with exceeding great joy. And when they were come into the house, they saw the young child with Mary his mother, and fell down, and worshipped him: and when they had opened their treasures, they presented unto him gifts; gold, and frankincense, and myrrh. And being warned of God in a dream that they should not return to Herod, they departed into their own country another way.

AND WHEN THEY WERE departed, behold, the angel of the Lord appeareth to Joseph in a dream, saying, Arise, and take the young child and his mother, and flee into Egypt, and be thou there until I bring thee word: for Herod will seek the young child to destroy him. When he arose, he took the young child and his mother by night, and departed into Egypt: And was there until the death of Herod: that it might be fulfilled which was spoken of the Lord by the prophet, saying, Out of Egypt have I called my son. . . . But when Herod was dead, behold, an angel of the Lord appeareth in a dream to Joseph in Egypt, Saying, Arise, and take the young child and his mother, and go into the land of Israel: for they are dead which sought the young child's life. And he arose, and took the young child and his mother, and came into the land of Israel. But when he heard that Archelaus did reign in Judaea in the room of his father Herod, he was afraid to go thither: notwithstanding, being warned of God in a dream, he turned aside into the parts of Galilee: And he came and dwelt in a city called Nazareth: that it might be fulfilled which was spoken by the prophets, He shall be called a Nazarene.

Memorial at Valley Forge

LOUISE WALKER

CHRISTMAS Day, 1776, found George Washington and his troops encamped on the west side of the Delaware River preparing to surprise the British. There were no Christmas songs or lights, no Christmas sights or sounds. "It is fearfully cold and raw and a snowstorm setting in," Washington described the day as he wrote in his diary at 6 P.M. "The wind is northeast and beats in the faces of the men. It will be a terrible night for the soldiers who have no shoes. Some of them have old rags tied around their feet, but I have not heard a man complain."

Bitter winds and snow and cold do indeed come to mind when we remember that Christmas 200 years ago. Washington's men crossed the Delaware River, as most of us remember from history books, and defeated the British, first at Trenton, and then on January 3rd, at Princeton. After these victories, events were unfavorable. The year 1777 brought defeat at the battles of Germantown and Brandywine. Clearly, the Americans were not ready to win the war: they were ill-equipped, poorly drilled, and they did not have the strength in arms and military prowess of the British. It seemed to many that the rule of Britain could not be shaken.

Today, worshipers in the Washington Memorial Chapel at Valley Forge are surrounded at Christmas by fragrant greens and candlelight and music. But that miserable winter is remembered. Memorials everywhere—in stained glass windows, in wood carvings, in flags and pennants—recall the soldiers' courage and strength of character, and the leadership of George Washington. The winter of Valley Forge is dramatically recorded there.

The Terrible Winter

George Washington had decided that rather than fight on in weakness, it would be wiser to select a place where his troops could rest and gain strength for a spring offensive. On December 19, 1777, nearly 11,000 men, raggedly dressed, hungry and weary, gathered at Gulph Mills to hear why they were going to Valley Forge, and to await orders to march the few miles to their destination. Washington thanked them for their patience and fortitude during the past year and promised them a winter free from fighting, but one in which they should expect to work hard. He had chosen this particular encampment because its location would not further crowd the hundreds of Patriots—citizens who had fled British-held Philadelphia. The natural layout of the land, which had once been the site of an old iron forge, was suitable for the intended purpose, and from this point they could keep a close eye on the enemy.

They were a pathetic sight—those men. On arrival at Valley Forge, Washington wrote in his journal: "The men sloshed through it [heavy rain]. You might have tracked the army from White Marsh to Gulph Mills to Valley Forge by the blood of their feet."

Looking around, the men must have realized what their leader meant by a winter of hard work. Valley Forge could scarcely be called a village, for it consisted of only a few scattered farmhouses, the forge, and a grist mill. The line of low hills did little to keep out the cold wind. The Schuylkill River and Valley Creek were freezing rapidly, but they would at least provide water.

The men's first task was to set up tents. Following that, hundreds of men were assigned to cut trees and hew logs so they could build more than 900 huts in which to live during the mid-winter months. Each hut would house 12 men and measured approximately 14 by 16 feet. Other men dug entrenchments, hoping they would be completed before the ground was deeply frozen. Because an early winter had set in, they tried to work speedily. But this was not easy for they were cold, hungry, and so poorly clad that many men wrapped their feet in rags because there were not enough shoes for all.

When the cold and hunger became almost unbearable, some of the men would start the chant, "no meat, no meat," and others would join the complaint. When Washington heard this he left his worktable in his headquarters to walk among the men. He made personal inquiries about their health; he asked if they had heard from their families; he assured them that he was trying to secure more supplies. Because they believed him, they stopped complaining—until they began to feel desperate again.

There was something about their commander in chief that strengthened those who came to know him. His sincerity and faithfulness in trying to carry out his promises to plead for more supplies are recorded in the never-ending stream of letters he wrote to the Continental Congress. He also wrote to various leaders who might facilitate shipments from France of heavy wool blankets and watch coats needed by the men on duty.

In mid-winter he wrote that only half the men had blankets and one-third were still without shoes, stockings, or breeches. In a letter dated January 5, 1778, he wrote: "As to meat, our stock is trifling, not being sufficient for more than two days." On February 5, he wrote to Governor Jonathan Trumbull about the "alarming situation of this army on account of provision. . . . There is strongest reason to believe that its existence cannot be of long duration, unless more constant, regular and larger supplies of meat . . . are furnished than have been for some time past. . . ." He wrote of the increasing sickness among the men. "Camp fever" became prevalent, and finally smallpox broke out. Men in hospitals had to lie on unsanitary straw beds which spread infection. By spring, 3,000 men were ill!

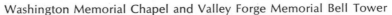

Washington Memorial Chapel and Valley Forge Memorial Bell Tower

Medallion in the George Washington Window ("The American"), showing Washington at prayer with Isaac Potts in background

"Sacrifice and Devotion" (Heckscher Memorial), in the garth adjoining the Cloister of the Colonies

Log cabin hut, such as those used by soldiers in winter of 1777-1778

The Man and His Faith

George Washington was an impressive figure, standing erect and just over six feet. Whether on foot or horseback, his bearing was aristocratic and dignified. It is said that when his gray-blue eyes looked straight into the eyes of another, they reflected both a fearless and a compassionate nature. He shared his men's discomforts, for he shared their suffering. He had known sickness (his face was pox-marked) and he had had malaria and pleurisy as a young man. At Valley Forge he contracted varioloid, a mild form of smallpox, which plagued many of the men.

Washington refused to accept a salary during the Revolution. Earlier, he chose to serve his country as an active member of the Virginia House of Burgesses and as a member of the Continental Congress, as well as working as a gentleman farmer on his large Virginia plantation.

He was a devoted church member, active in the Protestant Episcopal Church from the time he accepted the office of vestryman at Truro Parish, Virginia, in 1762. From his mother it is said he learned to love the Bible and the Book of Common Prayer, and he taught Christian precepts through Bible reading and prayer in his own home. On Sunday afternoons the family set aside an hour to read the Bible and discuss verses that had special meaning for them. Frequently, he composed and wrote out prayers for personal or public use.

Because prayer was a vital part of his life, several stories have grown up about Washington at prayer. One of these, which may or may not be legendary, is depicted in a medallion in the George Washington window at Valley Forge. It shows Isaac Potts, a Quaker who offered his farm home to Washington for headquarters, coming upon the commander in chief at prayer. It was apparently Washington's custom to go to a secluded place in the woods where he might be quite alone. On one such occasion, the account goes, Isaac Potts happened to be out riding when he dismounted and stood quietly beside his horse. Hearing a voice, he looked around and saw George Washington kneeling, absorbed at prayer.

This is one of several stories that support the idea that Washington believed in the power of prayer, and that Christianity was part of his daily life. He urged his men to fast and pray, and on occasion, issued orders through the Continental Congress for "days of fasting, humiliation, and prayer." After he became president of the United States, he continued his custom of asking a blessing at meals. Sunday visitors were invited to attend church with the president and his family. Even in the most demanding days of his life, it is said that he went to church and daily observed a time of private prayer.

At Valley Forge, and elsewhere when with his men, he allowed no profanity or gambling among the troops. When a chaplain was in camp, he would announce that divine services would be held and the officers and men were expected to attend unless they were ill or on special duty.

George Washington's character is sensitively portrayed in a statue near the lectern of the Washington Memorial Chapel. Done in bronze by Franklin Simmons, the work is titled "Valley Forge." Washington is seated, weary and thoughtful. His sword lies across his knees to symbolize that there was no fighting at Valley Forge during the encampment. His face is

"Valley Forge"
by Franklin Simmons

16

etched with deep anxiety to signify that he bears the burdens of his men and nation. The face—indeed, the entire posture of the figure—gives the impression that here is a man of strength, confidence, and hope.

The Washington Memorial Chapel

Valley Forge today is both a lovely park and a memorial in the form of a chapel, nearly every part of which recalls the winter of 1777-1778, and our nation's struggle for independence. In the park there are markings to indicate the lines of entrenchments; there are several replicas of the huts; the drill grounds are marked off; and Isaac Potts' home, which served as Washington's headquarters, is restored with furnishings of 200 years ago.

The founding of the Washington Memorial Chapel goes back to 1903 when, on Washington's birthday, the Reverend W. Herbert Burk, rector of All Saints Episcopal Church in Norristown, urged in his sermon that a memorial chapel be built at Valley Forge. The idea caught on, and the edifice was completed in 1917. The chapel has always been a Protestant Episcopal Church maintained by freewill offerings of members and visitors, together with generous and creative gifts and labor from patriotic organizations.

The architectural style of the chapel is Gothic, so that when one first enters, the impression is that of being in a small, jewel-like, French or English style Gothic cathedral. Whether the day is cloudy or sunny, the predominately red and blue stained glass windows glow and sparkle like the windows in Chartres Cathedral. Dr. Burk had instructed the D'Ascenzo Studio to have red predominate in one window and blue in the next. With the light walls between, the national colors are seen throughout the chapel.

All the windows were designed and created by the late Nicola D'Ascenzo in his Philadelphia studio. He used an overall theme, "Abundant Life through Jesus Christ," developing the idea that this quality of life comes through service and sacrifice.

Over the altar is the marvelous window given by the Pennsylvania Society of the Colonial Dames of America in memory of Martha Washington. It is based on our Lord's word, "I am come that they might have life, and that they might have it more abundantly." In the center is the crucifixion, and above it are the three Marys bringing the Easter message. In the lower openings the institutions of the family, the church, and the nation are represented, concluding with religion, science, and at the extreme right, art, which is represented by architecture, sculpture, painting, and music.

Over the front entrance is the George Washington window, given by the Pennsylvania State Society of the Daughters of the American Revolution. Through a series of medallions, 36 scenes from Washington's life are depicted. The first scene shows his baptism; then he is pictured as a young student; later, he is in his first occupation as a surveyor. The sequence of

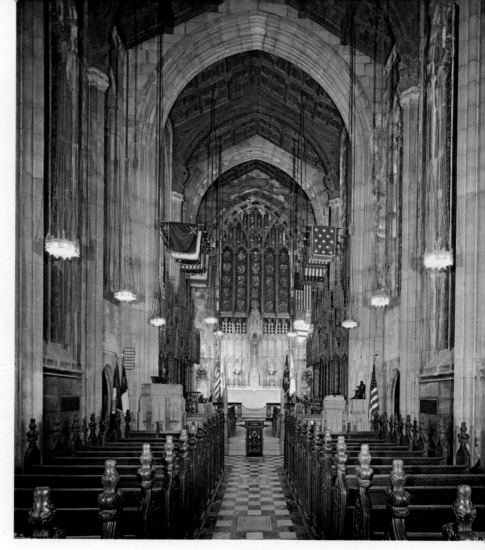

Nave of the Washington Memorial Chapel

his military life is depicted through his first defeat, and then as he presides at the funeral service of General Braddock at Fort Duquesne. His marriage to Martha Danbridge is pictured in two medallions. He is shown leaving for the Continental Army. Then follow several scenes of victories over the British. There is the quiet scene of Washington at prayer in the wooded grove at Valley Forge, with Isaac Potts and his horse standing a short distance away. Other events at Valley Forge are portrayed which lead finally to the victory at Yorktown, Virginia. The last ten medallions, with the theme of peace on earth, are concerned with Washington's service to his country as president. The last of these shows Washington reading the Bible at the close of day at Mount Vernon.

There are 13 windows in all, beginning with the great Christ window, as the Martha Washington Memorial Window is often called. The others are placed in the following order: Carrying the Gospel to the Ends of the Earth, The New Birth and the New Freedom, Freedom through the Word, Discovery, Settlement, Expansion, Development, Revolution, Patriotism, Democracy, The Union, and The George Washington Memorial Window, sometimes spoken of as "The American."

The windows along each side of the nave carry out the general themes as mentioned, each relating to a leader in the early history of America. There is Bishop White's window which recalls the history of the English church. (Bishop White, the first bishop of Penn-

17

sylvania, played an important part in bringing the gospel to America.) The Alexander Hamilton window has for its theme "Freedom through Truth"; the Benjamin Franklin window, "Freedom through the Word"; Nathanael Greene, "The Window of Discovery"; Lafayette, "The Window of Settlement"; General Anthony Wayne, "The Window of Expansion"; Robert Morris, "The Window of Development"; John Paul Jones and Richard Dale, "The Window of the Revolution." Of particular interest in recalling the winter at Valley Forge are scenes in this window showing the huts, Martha Washington caring for a sick soldier, and the celebration of the French Alliance at Valley Forge. Completing the cycle are "The Window of Patriotism," "The Window of Democracy," and "The Window of Union."

Valley Forge Memorial Bell Tower

Important and impressive as the windows may be, there is a rich variety of wood carvings to tell the story of the winter at Valley Forge. On each end, the choir stalls have a figure of a revolutionary soldier kneeling in prayer. Inscriptions are carved on the backs of several of the choir stalls. Much of the wood carving, including the prayer desk at the foot of the chancel steps, was done by Edward Maene, a Belgian who came to live in Philadelphia. The pews are called the "Pews of the Patriots," commemorating a patriot or group of patriots. Typical of the carving on the

backs of pews and choir stalls is the carving on the Benjamin Franklin Memorial pew, an admonition said to have been given by Franklin to his daughter: "Go constantly to church. The act of devotion in the Common Prayer Book is your principal business there, and if properly attended to, will do more towards amending the heart than sermons generally do. I wish you would never miss the prayer days."

The chapel contains scores of flags and shields, among them early state flags and regimental colors and the army and navy flags of the Revolution. Suspended from the right wall of the chancel is a shield-shaped flag which bears the Washington family coat of arms. On its white background are three red stars placed above two wide red stripes.

Commemorative tablets, plaques, and inscriptions abound. The painted ceiling of the chapel is known as "The Roof of the Republic." It displays the state seals in the order the states entered the Union.

Outside, to the left and west of the chapel, is the lovely stone carved "Cloister of the Colonies." Each of the arched bays represents one of the 13 original colonies. "The Porch of the Allies," to the right and east of the chapel, honors men from European countries who helped the cause of the Continental Army: Major General Von Steuben, drillmaster, and Gen-

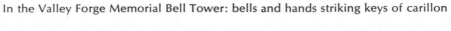

In the Valley Forge Memorial Bell Tower: bells and hands striking keys of carillon

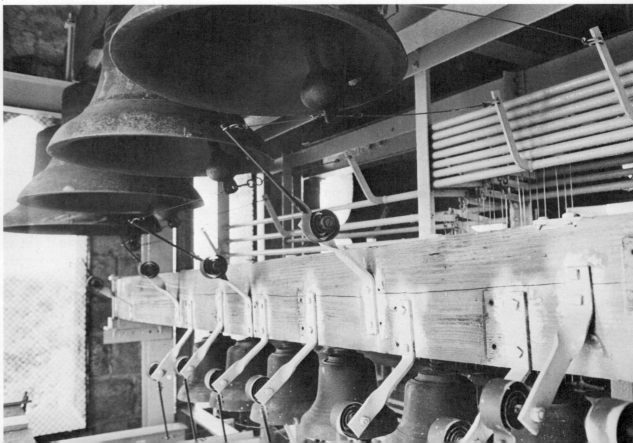

eral Johann DeKalb, both from Germany; General Lafayette from France, and General Rochambeau, whose salary was contributed by France; and General Pulaski from Poland.

The bell tower, standing as a separate structure just east of the chapel, houses the Washington Memorial National Carillon. It rises 100 feet above ground level and contains a carillon of 58 cast bells. There is one bell for each of the states; one for Washington, D.C.; one for each of these territories: the Virgin Islands, Puerto Rico, Guam, American Samoa, Midway, and Wake Island; and finally, a National Birthday Bell. Frank Pechin Law, internationally recognized carillonneur, began to play the original "Peace Chime," as the first bells were called, when he was taught while quite young to play simple melodies. In 1953, the present carillon and tower were completed and dedicated by the National Society, Daughters of the American Revolution. During the entire year, but more often in the summer months, Mr. Law, and other leading carillonneurs of the world, give recitals on this carillon which has been pronounced second to none.

Visitors usually step into the open area of the tower at ground level and look up at the shimmering rose window which pictures Washington at prayer in Valley Forge. This window was designed by David Bramnick of Philadelphia and executed by the D'Ascenzo Studios. (The design of this window is not the same as that of the small medallion showing Washington at prayer in the Washington window over the main entrance to the chapel, although the setting appears to be the grove of trees where Washington is said to have retired to pray at Valley Forge.) The rose window in the tower pictures the commander in chief alone in the woods and around this central scene are symbols of the Washington family. Eight trefoil designs extend from the circular center, four containing symbols of the four apostles and alternating with four French fleur-de-lis that honor the assistance France gave to America during the Revolution.

Below the window and running along the side walls is a frieze, sculptured in low relief. It was given by the Children of the American Revolution. It highlights the history of Valley Forge, showing the coming of the Continental Army, the building of the huts and entrenchments, and other events that climaxed in Evacuation Day, June 18, 1778, when the first division of the army left to join forces under General Wayne. This led eventually to ultimate victory over the British.

The Reverend Sheldon Moody Smith, the present rector of the chapel, succeeding the second rector, the Reverend John Robbins Hart, describes Christmas at the chapel, from its very beginning, as a time when candles glow, choirs sing, and music of the organ fills the church. Bells from the carillon ring out over the park.

The Cloister of the Colonies

As worshipers quietly leave the chapel, passing down the aisles and through the great entrance just beyond the George Washington window, they pause to look out over the peaceful countryside that stretches ahead. In the distance the Schuylkill River and Valley Creek outline two sides of the park. Beauty and tranquility are everywhere in the 2,255 acres of low, gently rolling hills—an area that once comprised drill grounds, avenues of log huts, and clusters of artillery. At a moment such as this, phrases of Washington's "Prayer for The United States of America" may come to mind. The words are a benediction, staying in one's memory because of the truth they have for all time.

> And finally that Thou wilt most graciously
> be pleased to dispose us all to do justice,
> to love mercy, and to demean
> ourselves with that
> charity, humility, and pacific temper
> of mind which were the characteristics of the
> Divine Author of our blessed religion,
> and without a humble imitation of whose
> example in these things we can never
> hope to be a happy nation.

The author wishes to thank Frank Pechin Law, carillonneur of the Washington Memorial National Carillon in Valley Forge, and John F. Reed, historian, for invaluable assistance in the preparation of this article.

A Declaration of Interdependence

ALVIN N. ROGNESS

THIS LAND is my land. I have no other. I think of my land and am filled with a full orchestration of emotions. I am proud. I am grateful. Reflecting on her history there surges through me a whole medley of feeling: hope, wonder, awe, remorse, indignation, fear, humor, sometimes even cynicism and bitterness. But the dominant chords are gratitude and hope.

I belong to this land.

I belong first to the God who gave me this land. Everything is his, every part of this vast universe. The three billions of people on the planet are his people. He created them and he redeemed them. To each one he has given a land. He has given me this land.

He has honored me with management, under him. He allows me to say "*my* family, *my* church, *my* farm, *my* school, *my* country." This great land, the United States of America, is mine to love, mine to care for, mine to govern, mine to use, mine to enjoy.

He does not leave us to our own resources alone. We live in the awareness and faith that he himself has invaded the earth. He came to Bethlehem soon 2000 years ago, with the angels' announcement that this coming would bring peace to men of goodwill.

Strange and incredible as this advent must seem by any dramatic standards of earth, the event of Christmas has done more to change the course of history than any other. The Son of God became the Son of man and for 33 years walked among men.

This is more than another myth of gods and goddesses mingling with the children of men. This is God entering history in the person of his Son, Jesus Christ, not on a little reconnaissance flight, but as the Lord of hosts. He came to engage and overcome the ancient enemy of man, to take into himself all the wretchedness, sin, and guilt of man, and by his death and resurrection, to remove the whole miserable cargo as far as the east is from the west.

This biblical story, beginning at the manger and moving through a cross to a resurrection and on to an ascension, has done more to release among men the great fruits of the Spirit—love, joy, peace, long-suffering, gentleness, goodness, faith—than all the laws of parliaments and rulers of the world. The story has unloosed the power of God among us.

It is in the promise of Jesus that he would never leave us nor forsake us that we make bold to assume management of the world for him.

A great number of our founding fathers derived their courage from this faith. The values reflected in the Declaration of Independence and in the Constitution emerge from this faith. We are profoundly affected by the Bethlehem child.

These Two Hundred Years

More change has been compressed into the last 200 years than in the cumulative history of man. For thousands of years, from Moses to George Washington, nothing had really changed in transportation, for instance. The fastest locomotion was a horse on a dry track, about 35 miles an hour. Now Pioneer 10, an odd, saucer-shaped $50 million spacecraft, has been hurtling through space for over two years, farther and faster than anything else made by man on its 500-million-mile journey to Jupiter. For hundreds of years the Chinese had black gunpowder, then came nitroglycerin 150 years ago, and then nuclear fission. Today we can devastate the earth in a day. For centuries the Orientals had the abacus, then came the adding machine, then electronics, with computers that add a million digits a second.

Is it any wonder that we stand transfixed between exhilaration and terror?

Must we believe that this unprecedented burst of knowledge and technology is the work of some demonic power plotting the destruction of man and his world? Or dare we believe that a great and good Creator has placed all these resources in the planet for man's good, that it is he who has given man the probing mind to ferret out these gifts, and that properly employed these discoveries can be for such benefit for the human race as we yet cannot imagine? I have grandchildren; I would like to believe that they may know a whole world of minimum drudgery and violence, a world much better than we have ever known.

I am proud that my country has been a pioneer and leader in this surge of invention and change, hazardous as the management of this power may be. What a stage our country has been for the drama of mind and will. Set free from political oppression, released for unrestrained experimentation, on these shores the mind of man has had full play.

A better future will not come about without the finest spiritual and moral efforts of man. God has chosen to work through people, not angels, to have his kingdom come to us on earth. If the high values of justice and mercy cannot govern our ways, creating freedom and opportunity for vast numbers of our people now oppressed by the very complexities of our technological society, perhaps God has minimal stake in the survival of our world. The ingenuity which produced our material culture, if it will concentrate on spiritual dimensions of life, may usher in a third century of triumphs in human values to compare with the technological triumphs of the first two. Without this turn, there may be no third century for our grandchildren.

Independence Hall
Philadelphia, Pennsylvania

A keepsake
American heritage
print

What of the Third Century?

There is a mood abroad that would give up on a future at all, settle for 200 years as the lifespan of the U.S.A., and sit around awaiting the quick and grim end of our civilization. This is the mood of cynicism.

Cynicism is the enemy. Nothing can emasculate us for the future as this can. And nothing is more demonic.

It feeds on distrust. We distrust our leaders, we distrust each other, and finally we give up any trust in God. It plunges us into severe panic or paralysis, or both.

The Constitution of our land is predicated on a profound biblical view of man and God. It presupposes realistically that people are not perfect, and it presupposes that God is active in the lives of people. Subject as man is to the evils of inordinate ambition, indulgence of self, indifference to others, ignorance, and the baser passions, he nonetheless is the object of God's creation and redemption. He has a conscience, and touched by God can defy the destructive drives within him and rise to heights of justice, mercy, integrity, and great efforts for the common good.

The Constitution could never have been written by cynical people. Dividing power among three departments of government, each with a check and balance on the other, recognizes the weakness and evil in men, and how the possession of power may destroy. But the document is permeated with high aspiration and hope. Justice is within reach and is possible because God has a stake in man and has not let him go.

Virtually every public address of our presidents, from Washington to Ford, reflects this nation's dependence on God. The court of highest appeal is not to some utilitarian humanism, but to the higher power, the transcendent, under whose law we stand to be judged and by whose mercy alone we dare to design a future. This note has always tempered the pride of our nation, tempted as we have been and are by the power which is ours.

We come to the close of 200 years of this government with the early dreams dimmed and the future unclear. The massive global issues that have surfaced —nuclear war, exhaustion of the planet's resources, communism, world hunger—these and others threaten us with a paralyzing fear and cynicism. A posture of hope for the future, so characteristic of our history, seems to falter, and with it a lethargy and indifference overtake us so alien to the spirit of enterprise which has made our nation strong and great.

More than any one thing needed to restore hope for the future is to recall man to the biblical faith of our fathers. An inventory of the achievements of two centuries will not do it. To believe that God has been at work among us, that despite our failures he does not abandon us, and that he has unpredictable resources available for our good, this alone will give us the courage to enter the third century with promise. This alone can defeat cynicism.

Reshaping a Dream

The American dream is a mosaic of many dreams. It is a dream that regarded this vast land as inexhaustible in resources. It thought of man as basically good. It prized vigor, initiative, boldness, and freedom as the prime virtues. It despised the aristocracy of birth and station. The man who could get the job done was the hero. The dream was never clearly defined and its parts were sometimes contradictory. But it had a powerful effect on the millions who came from across the oceans. It captured them with its optimism, its glow, and its promise.

But the dream had its dark underside. Neither the American Indian nor the black slave knew anything of its glow. Great numbers who remained the serfs of industry missed the dream's epic sweep. Others, unable to cope with the rugged competition of our individualism, remained a disillusioned fringe. And the growing complexities of our government and industrial structures make freedom for the individual a fading piece of the dream.

We come to the threshold of our third century deeply aware that the original dream must be amended if it shall serve a new day for our great country. Freedom can no longer mean freedom to do willy-nilly what we want to do; it must mean freedom to do what we ought to do, whatever that may do to the rugged individualism which served us well in a frontier age. Equality of opportunity must be translated into equality of results. Private enterprise must expand its responsibility vastly to include the public good.

Reshaping the dream for the next century will usher in a new constellation of virtues and values. This will require of our leaders and of us all greater wisdom and greater self-sacrifice than were demanded in the initial dream. Competition must be seasoned with cooperation, initiative with integrity, success with compassion.

What a pity if we yield to a prevailing mood of defeatism and give up dreaming altogether. We are descendants and heirs of people who spurned the hardships of the wilderness, who gave their lives for political self-determination, who welcomed change and risk as opportunity, who built a magnificent technical civilization, and who reached out to set foot on the moon. Dare we surrender to fear and lassitude? Must not we, as they, embrace the whole frontier as ours, this time too a frontier awaiting exploration and development, the frontier of great humanitarian values for Americans and for the entire world? Then we will indeed be a nation "under God."

A Declaration of Interdependence

We have long since given up the comfort of the Monroe Doctrine. It took my grandfather eight weeks to cross the Atlantic; we cross it in less than eight hours. News of a riot in Paris would have reached my grandfather in perhaps three weeks, and then through

The
First Prayer in Congress

by the Rev. J. Duche

O Lord, our Heavenly Father, High and Mighty King of Kings, and Lord of Lords, who dost from Thy throne behold all the dwellers on earth, and reignest with power supreme and uncontrolled over all the Kingdoms, Empires and Governments; look down in mercy we beseech Thee, on these American States, who have fled to Thee from the rod of the oppressor, and thrown themselves on Thy gracious protection, desiring hence forth to be dependent only on Thee; to Thee, they have appealed for the righteousness of their cause; to Thee do they now look up for that countenance and support which Thou alone canst give; take them therefore Heavenly Father, under Thy nurturing care; give them wisdom in Council and valor in the field; defeat the malicious designs of our cruel adversaries; convince them of the unrighteousness of their cause; and if they persist in their sanguinary purpose, O, let the voice of Thy own unerring justice, sounding in their hearts, constrain them to drop the weapons of war from their unnerved hands in the day of battle! Be Thou present, O God of wisdom, and direct the councils of this honorable assembly; enable them to settle things on the best and surest foundation, That the scene of blood may be speedily closed; that order, harmony and peace may be effectually restored, and truth and justice, religion and piety prevail and flourish among Thy people. Preserve the health of their bodies and vigor of their minds; shower down on them and the millions they here represent, such temporal blessings as Thou seest expedient for them in this world, and crown them with everlasting glory in the world to come. All this we ask in the name and through the merits of Jesus Christ, Thy Son, Our Savior.

Amen

Four score and seven years ago our fathers brought forth on this continent, a new nation, conceived in Liberty, and dedicated to the proposition that all men are created equal.

Now we are engaged in a great civil war, testing whether that nation, or any nation so conceived and so dedicated, can long endure. We are met on a great battlefield of that war. We have come to dedicate a portion of that field, as a final resting place for those who here gave their lives that that nation might live. It is altogether fitting and proper that we should do this.

But, in a larger sense, we can not dedicate — we can not consecrate — we can not hallow — this ground. The brave men, living and dead, who struggled here have consecrated it, far above our poor power to add or detract. The world will little note, nor long remember what we say here, but it can never forget what they did here. It is for us the living, rather, to be dedicated here to the unfinished work which they who fought here have thus far so nobly advanced. It is rather for us to be here dedicated to the great task remaining before us — that from these honored dead we take increased devotion to that cause for which they gave the last full measure of devotion — that we here highly resolve that these dead shall not have died in vain — that this nation, under God, shall have a new birth of freedom — and that government of the people, by the people, for the people, shall not perish from the earth.

Abraham Lincoln.

November 19, 1863.

---

a newspaper without pictures; today a little skirmish in any part of the world is on my TV screen while it happens. Our world is a very small island in space, every part linked to every other part with a subtile web of interdependence.

The third century will tax the statesmanship of the nations as never before, not primarily to have one nation survive at the expense of another, but to have the planet itself survive. The task is as simple and as sobering as that.

This does not mean that I love my country less. It means rather that in loving my own country I can better understand that others may love their countries as I do mine, and that with such understanding I may be willing to support my national leaders in a foreign policy which, at whatever material cost to my country, will move the entire world to goals of equality and peace. Never again is it possible for nations to say, "You leave us alone and we will leave you alone." The rugged individualism so important for our national development in the past can in the future be as destructive as once it was constructive.

The supreme political issue ultimately is world peace. Nor can this be achieved by a balance of terror. At this moment the United States and the Soviet Union, between them, possess nuclear stockpiles in excess of 75,000 megatons of explosive force. If only one-fourth of this power were to be used, a blanket of deadly radioactivity could settle over the globe. Thousands of years of civilization could be gone almost overnight.

It will take a radical reorientation for us, from independence to interdependence, if as people who love our land we can marshall the kind of public opinion and pressure that will support our national leaders as they shape a foreign policy innovative enough to avert disaster.

And may it not be that vital to such a vision will be a recovery of our elemental Christian faith which makes of all people everywhere the world over our brothers and neighbors? Jesus drew the whole, hurting world into his heart and said, "Whatever you do for them, you have done to me."

The Lord of All Nations

The Christian faith that has dominated the life of our country is not a tribal or national religion. From the beginning Jesus instructed his followers to claim the whole world for him. And why shouldn't they? It is his world. He created it and he redeemed it. He is Lord of all.

Before the first century was over his followers had fanned out into the entire Mediterranean world. This was more than a Judean sect. This was a faith for all the world.

Our Lord has always been an internationalist. He belongs to no one continent or race. We cherish him in our own national history, but our country has sent thousands of its citizens to all parts of the earth with the story of Jesus and his claim of Lordship. There has been no Monroe Doctrine in the Christian church.

And today, when the nations of the world need some unifying symbol, some common allegiance, something or Someone who can command their admiration, loyalty, and even adoration, without destroying the rich diversities of their many cultures, who is there but this Galilean, this Child of Bethlehem? Pontius Pilate's verdict, "I find no fault in him," has been, and continues to be, the universal verdict of the ages the world over.

We who claim him as Lord and Savior present him as the Lord of all the nations. He it is who can bring peace to all men of good will.

24

Abraham Lincoln at Gettysburg

A keepsake
American heritage
print

Bruton Parish Church in winter

Christmas in Colonial Williamsburg

A Walk Through Time

JEAN LOUISE SMITH

TO WALK down mile-long Duke of Gloucester Street in Williamsburg, Virginia, during the Christmas season, is to discover today something of the life and times of colonial Williamsburg more than 200 years ago. Imagination makes that journey in time easily, for all around are things of the past to see, hear, smell, and taste. The sense of touch is a part of the journey too, not so much through the hands as through the heart and mind.

The sight of old homes, taverns, and shops quickly puts the visitor back into colonial times. Houses and shops were constructed of brick or wood and painted in a variety of colors. Public buildings such as the capitol and the Governor's Palace were made of brick. Historic Williamsburg is similar to an old English town transplanted in America. It reminds us that, for many years, the colony of Virginia was indeed English.

Whether or not there is snow at Christmas in colonial Williamsburg, there is no mistaking the season on Duke of Gloucester Street in December. The doorways of every home and shop, the Palace and the capitol, are wreathed and garlanded with handsome holiday decorations. In this, a plastic age, all-natural decorations are a delight to see.

Evening comes, and with it every window in town is lighted by a single candle. On the green that is called the Market Square, stands a community Christmas tree with white lights, and often, close by, a bonfire or two burns so that those who stroll up and down the street may warm themselves.

There are sounds of Christmas, too. Costumed carolers perform several times during the season, singing well-loved English carols. The women and girls wear capes over full skirts, and the men and boys

27

The capitol building at colonial Williamsburg

wear tricornered hats and knee breeches. Sometimes their singing is accompanied by 18th century instruments. The brisk music of a fife and drum corps may sound the opening of some special program at one of the historic buildings. Other musicians perform at the Williamsburg Lodge or at taverns where they take part in entertaining guests who throng to Williamsburg at the Christmas season. Visitors, also part of the sight and sound of the Historic Area, are orderly, appreciative people of all ages, who really enjoy being caught up and surrounded by the atmosphere and activities this gracious setting affords.

What of the smells of Christmas at Williamsburg? To those who come from the North, the first delicate fragrance is that of growing greens. Leaves have fallen from the deciduous trees, but much greenery remains: bayberry with its spicy odor, boxwood, and mountain laurel. Waxy magnolia leaves remain on the trees in abundance. These greens are used for decorations, as are others which include holly and mistletoe. Here and there flowers linger to delight the eye. Frequent rains keep the air sweet with the delicious smell of trees and shrubs.

Another distinctive scent, infrequently experienced by today's city dweller, comes from wood-burning fires. Every home, tavern, and inn has at least one fireplace, and most have several. In Williamsburg, wood fires are kept burning both for warmth and atmosphere. Indoors and out, their pungent odor is present.

And taste! A meal at Williamsburg at Christmastime, whether in the coffee shop of the Lodge or at one of the historic taverns, becomes a gastronomic adventure. If one chooses to order any of the special

28

dishes, there are treats such as smoked Virginia ham, game pie, and a variety of seafoods from the Chesapeake Bay. There is English trifle, tipsy squire, plum pudding—the list of special foods is long. The "Groaning Board Feast," the "Old Dominion Dinner," and the "Plantation Breakfast" are all occasions when taste is paramount. Old recipes are used, and local foods are featured.

The walk through time that persons make today at Williamsburg in the Christmas season is redolent with feeling. Depending on the individual, these feelings may be nostalgic, spiritual, filled with joy, or they may simply be a response to beauty. These are responses to concerts attended in candlelit rooms and to worship services in old Bruton Parish Church. Children feel joy as they enter into games and contests of long ago. These take place at the Palace when costumed children show visitors how to do the sack race, English penny pitching, and roll hoops and barrels. Visiting children need no help in competing in a pie-eating contest or watching a puppet show. Families and singles enjoy the yule log ceremony at the Lodge on Christmas Eve, the procession of the Wassail Bowl, and other special events.

Christmas at Williamsburg lasts from mid-December through New Year's Day. Visitors come for long or short periods; many make reservations for the coming year when they are checking out, for it is virtually impossible to get accommodations at short notice.

To experience time spent at Williamsburg at Christmas or at any season of the year is to wonder how the restoration came about; it is to reflect on why this town is important in the early history of our nation. To make these discoveries, we need to go back in

Carolers sing as they stroll the streets during the Christmas season

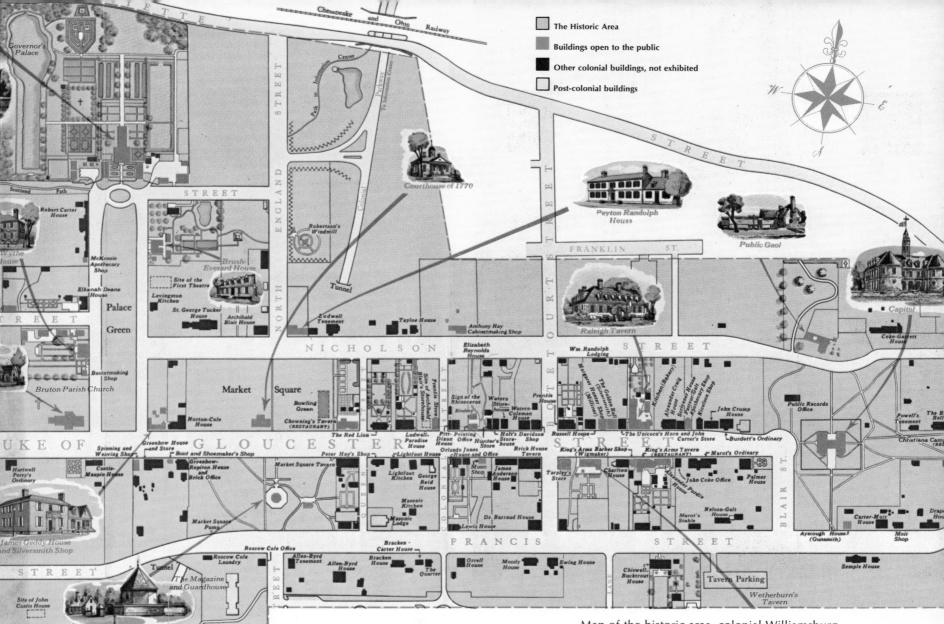

time to the fall of 1926 when John D. Rockefeller Jr. went to the College of William and Mary to attend a meeting of the Phi Beta Kappa Society. There, he met with the Reverend Dr. W. A. R. Goodwin, rector of Bruton Parish Church, who had told him earlier of his dream of a restored colonial village.

In the mid-twenties, Williamsburg was a sleepy, even shabby town, except for the campus of the College of William and Mary. The decline had come about gradually after the capital of Virginia was moved to Richmond in 1780. So it was that when Mr. Rockefeller and Dr. Goodwin met at Williamsburg, they walked about, looked at the old houses and discussed how each might be restored to its former dignity and beauty. They gazed at the site where the stately Governor's Palace had once stood and talked about how it might be reconstructed if old drawings, artifacts, and descriptions could be found to make the reconstruction authentic. They agreed that if the project were to be undertaken, the town must be preserved and authentically reconstructed. This walk was later referred to as "the most expensive walk in history."

A year later Mr. Rockefeller founded an organization to begin the enormous task. It became the forerunner of the present-day foundation which administers the continuing work of the restoration, the non-profit, educational institution known as The Colonial Williamsburg Foundation.

Mr. Rockefeller gave his personal attention and resources unstintingly to the work of the foundation. There were nearly 100 original structures to be restored as well as several important buildings that needed to be reconstructed after painstaking archeological research. These, together with the planting of some 90 acres of 18th century gardens and greens, comprised the enormous task which was undertaken.

The work continued over many years and is still going on whenever old records and findings come to light. During those early years of restoration there was an abundance of help for making everything authentic. One of the largest tasks was researching and rebuilding the Governor's Palace which had burned to the ground just after the victory at Yorktown which ended the Revolutionary War. Archeologists, sifting beneath the ground near the old palace, found pieces of marble, tile, wood carvings, hardware, and other clues that enabled them to reconstruct a replica of the original palace. In other places—even in England—researchers found letters, diaries, old newspapers, and drawings which assisted the team of archeologists, architects, historians, and landscape architects who reconstructed the palace with its complex of buildings and extensive gardens. Almost all

29

Dining room at the George Wythe Home, with Christmas decorations

separate building a few feet from the house itself. Each house usually had a stable, a well, a dairy, smokehouse, laundry, servants quarters, and what was delicately referred to as "the necessary house." These complexes of homes with their outbuildings have been carefully restored and outfitted with authentic furnishings and equipment of their period. The journals, account books, and inventories which many families kept, proved to be of great value to the restorers.

The shops and taverns along Duke of Gloucester Street, as well as the residences, are beautifully decorated at Christmas in a manner derived from the 18th century. Each year there is a contest among the residents—most of whom are staff members of the foundation—for door decorations, the basic rule being that only natural, growing things may be used. Garlands and wreaths of live greens are enhanced in the Della Robbia manner with apples, lemons, pineapple, and other fruits, as well as with pine cones, holly, and red berries. In the exhibition building decorations are placed around doorways, in windows, on lamp posts, and inside the period rooms, faithfully furnished with American and English antiques. The dining room table in each home is usually set with old silver, china, and linen, set off by a Christmas centerpiece. Seeing these homes and public places recalls something of the Christmas festivities of 250 years ago in England and America when hanging the greens was all-important.

The handcraft displays in Williamsburg fascinate today's visitors at any time of the year, but they have a special interest at Christmas, when thoughts are on making and giving gifts. In the 18th century, journeymen and master craftsmen came to Williamsburg to make articles such as cabinets, barrels, guns,

Costumed carolers in the historic area

of the work on the palace was accomplished between December, 1931, and April, 1934.

The fact that old Williamsburg was a planned town (the plan was drawn up in 1699 when the capital was moved from Jamestown) helped in its restoration. The historic area today includes 175 acres of the earlier town. The original plan, still in existence, shows the mile-long Duke of Gloucester Street with the Wren Building (1695) of the College of William and Mary at the western end of the avenue and the capitol at the eastern end. Duke of Gloucester Street was 99 feet wide, lined by fine old houses, large and small, and by shops and taverns which also served as hotels. Green space was important to any town in those early days, and the plan included a large green, usually referred to as the Market Square. In addition there were some 90 acres of gardens around the homes. These green spaces and gardens have been restored or reconstructed as closely as possible to their original state.

Because Williamsburg was more of a rural town than a city, every home had a vegetable garden and some fruit trees. Nearly every family kept a few animals since one or more horses were necessary for transportation. A cow, a pig or two, chickens, and perhaps ducks, geese, and a goat would be added. In colonial Virginia most families kept servants and slaves. The work of sustaining a family went on in buildings outside the house. The kitchen was in a

clocks, and musical instruments. These men usually took apprentices from the general populace, and occasionally one of them would decide to remain in the town. Men and women and older children in a family engaged in crafts along with their regular household and civic duties. They spun wool and wove it on looms into cloth; they ground meal and baked bread; they made harnesses. Most of the villagers looked to shop keepers for specialized goods and services such as wigs and wig-dressing, boots and shoes, millinery, medicine and herb products. Today, in the several shops on Duke of Gloucester Street, costumed persons work at crafts, using the tools and methods of colonial days. In each of these places there are men and women who act as hosts and hostesses, explaining the craft and offering historical orientation.

King Charles II referred to Virginia as "The Old Dominion." Early on, the colonists themselves called the area where the town of Williamsburg now stands, "Middle Plantation," before they renamed it in honor of King William III. Life in those days centered around the institution of the plantation, which was in itself a small business. George Washington owned a plantation in Virginia, and he took the responsibility of running it seriously. At the same time, he served as a member of the House of Burgesses for 16 years and as a vestryman in Truro Parish Church. Now, at Carter's Grove Plantation, a few miles from Williamsburg, one can get an idea of what plantation life was like.

There are many reasons why Williamsburg was important in the developing history of our country. For one thing, the colonists had a strong concept of the importance and integrity of the individual. They believed in self-government and in taking part in civic and governmental affairs even when personal business might be pressing. They were determined to establish a new life in the land to which they had come. They worked hard to keep these ideals and put them into practice.

In 1765, when England passed the Stamp Act which imposed intolerable taxes on the colonists, most of the people supported Patrick Henry after he gave his fiery speech at the capitol in Williamsburg. Following this, a group of Patriots in the House of Burgesses approved a document written by George Mason known as the Virginia Declaration of Rights. In 1776, it was adopted unanimously by the legislators who had assembled at the capitol. The 16 articles, which set forth fundamental human rights, were highly influential in drafting the first 10 amendments of the Constitution of the United States. The Proclamation of the Declaration of Independence, which set off the Revolution, was quickly supported by the Virginia Colony. From then on, Williamsburg began to lose its English characteristics and loyalty.

Nonetheless, a good deal of England left its stamp on Williamsburg as is evident today in the restored area. For many years the king's representative lived

The kitchen at Carter's Grove Plantation, decorated for Christmas

at the Governor's Palace and set the pace for an English style of society. It was an important post, for Virginia was Britain's largest American colony, stretching west to the Mississippi River and north to the Great Lakes. The very size of the colony made it an empire of which Britain was proud. Also important to Virginia as an English colony was the town of Jamestown, just eight miles from Williamsburg, where the first permanent English settlement was established in the New World in 1607. There, in Festival Park, full-scale replicas of the ships that brought the settlers to America are displayed: the *Susan Constant*, the *Discovery*, and the *Godspeed*. They sailed

The 18th century Market Square Tavern, decked with evergreens

Governor's Palace, garlanded with Christmas greens

from London, December 20, 1606, and arrived at the place they named Jamestown on May 13, 1607.

The final battle of the War of Independence was fought at Yorktown, just 12 miles from Williamsburg. Both Jamestown and Yorktown, so important historically, may be visited from Williamsburg.

Many visitors to Williamsburg feel the beauty and wonder of Christmas at the Abby Aldrich Rockefeller Folk Art Collection. This small and exquisite museum is housed in an early 19th century style building that seems more like a home than a museum. The late Mrs. John D. Rockefeller Jr. gave more than 1500 works of American folk art for the museum, and at Christmas the most appropriate of these are displayed in a setting of greens, music, and reminders of the season as it was celebrated in America in the 19th century. A doll house, many antique toys, paintings, wood and metal objects of long ago are displayed. Each year a special theme is used throughout the museum — most recently this was "Christmas in the Southern Mountains." A large Christmas tree (called a mountaineer's tree) stood in the foyer. All of the decorations were handmade and could be created in mountain homes: strings of popcorn, tiny red peppers, and very small pinecones; cornshuck dolls, stuffed calico animals, and other unusual trimmings.

In the galleries the theme of Southern Mountain folklore was further explored in exhibitions of

Sconce with holly and red ribbon

hand-crafted primitive dolls and toys: a mountain cabin room, a barn with a carousel horse, duck decoys, and other animals. Christmas legends of the Southern Mountains tell of animals talking on Christmas Eve and that fire must burn all through the Christmas season.

Those who look for the sacredness and beauty of Christmas will want to return again and again to Bruton Parish Church. The oldest part of the present structure was completed in 1715. The first parish church was built in the mid-17th century; it was replaced by a larger church in 1683 that served both the College of William and Mary and the community for about 30 years. In the days before America won her independence, Bruton Parish Church was Anglican, closely related to the Crown, as was the Church of England. Since that time, it has been a parish church in the Episcopal Diocese of Southern Virginia. The present rector is the Reverend Cotesworth Pinckney Lewis, D.D.

Bruton Parish Church is rich in history and contains such treasures of the past as the Jamestown communion silver which dates from 1661, the pew honoring George Washington, and a 450-pound bell given to the church in 1761 by James Tarpley, a local merchant. The bell was cast in London by the Whitechapel Bell Foundry, the same firm that made the Liberty Bell in Philadelphia. It is still in active use. Notable persons worshiped in Bruton Parish Church, some of whom are buried in its churchyard.

Parishioners decorate their church with garlands of greens that are draped along the galleries. Della Robbia wreaths and large swatches of greens are hung from moldings and from wall light brackets each of which contains a glass-shielded candle. The poinsettias massed at the altar are breathtaking. They are arranged so that they do not hide the reredos on which are tablets inscribed with the Ten Commandments, the Lord's Prayer, and the Apostles' Creed. Services of worship, and choir and instrumental concerts are held frequently during the Christmas season, sometimes by candlelight. Candles along the wall give a soft, flickering glow as worshipers enter to pray and sing and hear the Christmas story. The music, by the choir, or on the organ or other musical instruments, is, for the most part, from the 18th century Baroque period.

Thousands of visitors who come to the church at Christmas must feel that they are walking through time as they are steeped in our early history. They celebrate the birth of the Child of Bethlehem in the knowledge that those who came to our country long ago in search of new life, may somehow be a part of today's search for the peace so longed for on earth!

Of Time and the Moment

Everything that happens
keeps on being a beginning,
and could it not be *His*
beginning, since beginning
is in itself so beautiful?

Rainer Maria Rilke
1875-1926

A new wind rises out of the hills
of America, and the song it
sings permeates the land.
It is a song of time and the moment.
It is a song of beginnings.

George Washington, the father of our country,
found a fount of new beginnings
when he knelt in prayer.
(Do we kneel today to ask for moments
that reveal some far horizon?)

Thomas Jefferson searched for an enduring
source of strength. And as he claimed
that source, it was a moment that became
for him a new beginning. "God who gave us
life gave us liberty," he said.
(Are we searching now for an enduring
source of strength?)

Abraham Lincoln heard the song the mighty
wind of freedom sings. The song became
articulate when the long dream he gathered in
his heart was shared and then came true.
" . . . This nation under God shall
have a new birth of freedom."
(Do we hold dreams that ask answering
deep in our hearts today?)

At Arlington, at every burying ground
where soldiers sleep, the wind is
but a whisper as it tells of memories.
Unnumbered crosses quietly proclaim that freedom
has been dearly bought to bring us
new beginnings.
(How do we honor those who gave
the gift of life?)

A new wind rises out of the hills
of America, and it sings of new beginnings.
We do not need new keys that open
to new worlds,
but old keys, making turns in
old familiar locks such as enduring
honesty, integrity, deep silences, and roots
of faith and hope and love.
Old keys, trusted and tried, that always open
to a world of new beginnings.

Oh, let a new wind rise
out of the hills of America—
now, at Christmas,
and as the old year turns.

—MELVA ROREM

33

Poems of Christmas

SHEPHERDS RETURNING

As they returned, climbing the rugged hill,
Were any sentences or phrases spoken,
Or were the gray-robed, sturdy shepherds still
With silence of the azure night unbroken
Except for sound of footsteps on the road?
Oh, surely after such a holy sight
They walked in silence on the stony sod,
And when at last within the country night
They reached the slumbering flocks, the lad who stayed
Upon the rocky slope to guard the sheep
Became aware of something great and wide,
A miracle of wonder vast and deep.
Oh, sometimes there are holy joys that reach
Beyond the farthest boundaries of speech!

GRACE V. WATKINS

FOR PASSERSBY

Basho, the poet, hung a gourd
outside his door in the lean times,
for those who wished him well
to leave small offerings of rice
    and other food.

My neighbor has reversed the role,
hanging on her apartment door
a fragrant wreath, from which we all
take bits of Christmas love and joy.

L. A. DAVIDSON

HERE IS A KING

Here is a King, this sleeping Child,
under God's brilliant, moving star.
For him we left the splendorous east,
asking, seeking, travelling far,

because we could not rest until
we found the place in which he lies,
sweet infant Lord among his beasts,
the love of God within his eyes.

We kneel before him, utter praise,
to Mary offer gold, and myrrh,
frankincense—tawdry gifts and poor
beside the Gift God gave to her—

(and when we go back to our lands,
in stealthy haste by secret ways,
the gladsome noise of angel choirs
will fall across our limpid days).

MARGARET STAVELY

THREE KINGS REMEMBER

We three remember when the cold winds blow
The endless days of weariness and strain
That we endured across the desert plain,
Seeking the Christ child, long and long ago.
We still can see the great star glowing bright—
The radiant star that burned across the sands—
Which led us, bearing gifts from distant lands,
Till we had found him on that winter's night.

Oh, still our hearts are warmed as we recall
The wondrous joy of that first Christmas morn
When we beheld the precious Baby, born
Of Mary, lying in the cattle stall.
And then we knew the Infant at her breast
Would bring men peace and give the weary rest.

WILLIAM ARNETTE WOFFORD

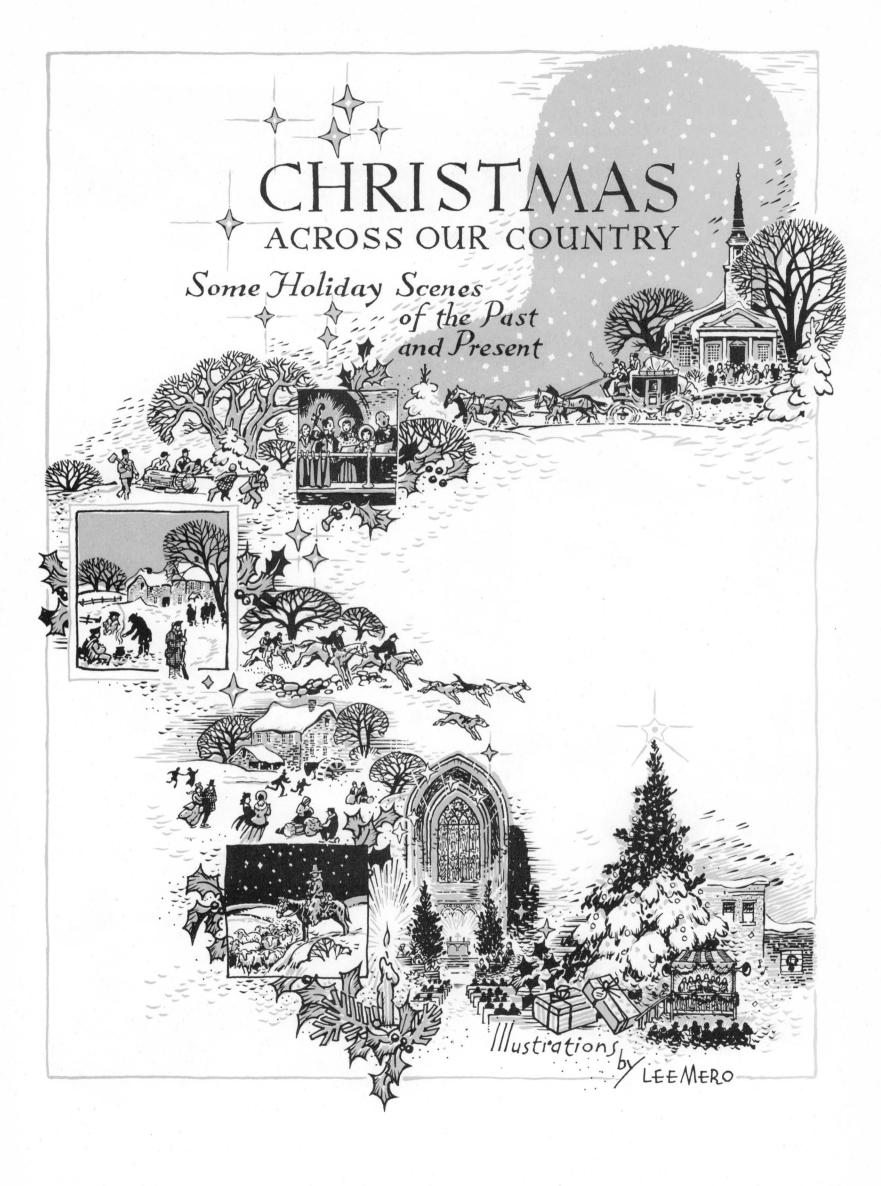

CHRISTMAS
ACROSS OUR COUNTRY

*Some Holiday Scenes
of the Past
and Present*

Illustrations by LEE MERO

The first Christmas celebration held by Englishmen in America was at Jamestown in 1607.

DOWN EAST

"The extreame winde, rayne, frost and snow caused us to keep Christmas among the salvages where we were never more merry, nor fed on more plenty of good Oysters, Fish, Flesh, Wildfowl and good Bread."

Smith's Spelling—not the artist's.

from the Record of Capt. John Smith

Christmas at Plymouth 1620

"We went on shore, some to fell timber, some to saw, some to rive, and some to carry; so no man rested all that day."

from Bradford's Record

There was dinner on the Mayflower in the evening—and "divers times."

In 1659 the General Court of Massachusetts deemed it necessary to enact this LAW!

"Whosoever shall be found observing any such day as Christmas or the like, either by forbearing of labor, feasting, or any other way as a festival shall be fined Five Shillings."

The Puritans regarded Christmas as a day of solemn worship.

In 1742, Nicolaus L. Zinzendorf arrived in Pennsylvania; Christmas Vigils were held in a stable and they named the place "BETHLEHEM".

first house, (with stable attached) Bethlehem Pa.

The Star of Bethlehem, (Pa.) today

By 1765, Christmas Travelers were beginning to have "Traffic Problems!"

ALBANY · NEW YORK

There were Travelers by the Boat Load on Christmas Night 1776!

From Painting by LEUTZE

Washington prayed with his troops at Valley Forge on Christmas Day, 1777

Christmas became a legal holiday in Massachusetts about the middle of the 18th century, and the day began to be celebrated in the real old English fashion around 1790 or the early 1800's.

There were "Hymns and prayer" in the morning

Boar's heads and Peacock Pies decorated the tables And Yule-logs burned in the Great Halls

TODAY, Municipal Christmas Trees brighten Public Squares

Soap-Bubble Parties were a popular Yuletide amusement in the 1880's and at Apple Bees young ladies found their future husband's initial when the peeling was coyly tossed over a shoulder!

Carols are sung on Beacon Hill (That's in Boston)

Gas Logs blaze for apartment dwellers

Covered Bridges of the Past now decorate modern Christmas Cards

Down South

Mistletoe is gathered

Back in the 1800's, a few days before Christmas, a load of cotton, behind a six mule hitch, would be decorated with colored streamers and sent to town to be traded for Holiday Supplies for the Plantation.

Riding to the Hounds on Christmas Day has always been popular

And River Packets carried folks back home for Christmas

Christmas Services have been held in the Bruton Parish Church Williamsburg, since 1715

In St. Louis, the Christmas Carols Association has a membership of over 30,000 singers

FIREWORKS are a Southern contribution to the American Christmas

Open house is the Custom at old Southern Mansions

An old plantation legend says that at the stroke of midnight, Christmas Eve, all the farm animals kneel toward the Star

Spanish moss provides unusual Christmas setting for a chapel Choir

There's skiing and ice-boating,
Folks skate on the
many lakes and rivers --
and the old-fashioned
bob-ride thrills the
youngsters during
the holidays.

MARJ
BEDE
KATHRYN

"Best Lighted Home"
contests are
sponsored by
Civic
Organizations

Candle Lighting Service is observed
in many Churches.

Carols are familiar to even
the smallest first-graders in country schools

WHITE CHRISTMAS
is the Rule, rather
than the Exception.

OUT WEST

A wagon Train brings supplies to Fort Clatsop on the Oregon Trail, Christmas, 1852.

Western Shepherd watches Flock

Shovel squad with SNO-CAT battles drifts on trail today

(Artist's note) A SNO-CAT is sno-relation to a TABBY-CAT —

Farolitos glow on adobe walls and Crèches appear in windows along the Santa Fe Trail.

In Altadena, California, Christmas Tree Lane is visited by thousands

In the Southwest, children are showered with candy and gifts when the "Piñata" is broken

Mission Workers endeavor to teach the Navajos the meaning of Christmas.

An inspiring service is held every Christmas at the base of the "Nation's Christmas Tree" in Sequoia National Park

(a requested reprint)

My Country ! 'tis of Thee

S.F. SMITH, 1830

H. CAREY 1743

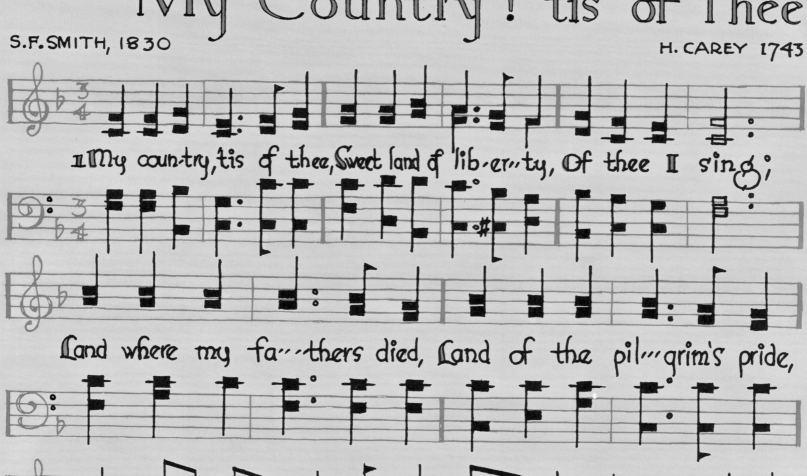

1 My country, 'tis of thee, Sweet land of lib-er-ty, Of thee I sing;

Land where my fa---thers died, Land of the pil---grim's pride,

From ev......'ry moun-tain side Let free---dom ring.

2 My native country, thee, Land of the noble, free, Thy name I love, I love thy rocks and rills, Thy woods and templed hills, My heart with rapture thrills like that above. 3 Let music swell the breeze. And ring from all the trees ✚ Sweet freedom's song; Let mortal tongues awake, Let all that breathe partake, Let rocks ⁛ their silence break, The sound prolong. 4 Our father's God, to Thee, Author of Liberty, to Thee we sing: Long may our land be bright with freedom's holy light; Protect us by Thy might Great God, our King. Amen.

THE LIBERTY BELL & INDEPENDENCE HALL

AMERICA

THE NATION'S CAPITOL WASHINGTON D.C.

Cathedral Bells

MELVA ROREM

CHRISTMAS joys may be increased for porcelain collectors! Today, and in the years to come, they may receive a gift from loved ones of Bing and Grøndahl's newest series of collectibles. A sculptured porcelain *Årsklokke,* Year Bell, five inches high and with a base opening four inches in diameter, is their most recent collector's treasure, a new one to be issued every year. It comes from Copenhagen, Denmark, and like other Bing and Grøndahl products, will have worldwide distribution.

Decorated in the traditional underglaze blue, it identifies with their popular Christmas, Jubilee, and Mother's Day plates, and with a charming variety of figurines. In numbers produced, the Year Bell is their most limited collector's item. Artists may make small changes in the shape of the bells through the years to make collecting more interesting.

Their plan is that each bell will honor a world-renowned cathedral. The first edition, offered in 1974,

features Roskilde Cathedral in Denmark; and the second bell, dated 1975, honors St. Peter's in the Vatican. Each clapper, made of brass and wood, rings out its singular tone, and the translucence of each bell's distinctive blue is enhanced by accents of 22-karat gold. On the outside of each bell we find the year, the cathedral's name, location, and silhouette—all in gold. On the inside the name and the year are reproduced in gold letters on a white surface, along with Bing and Grøndahl's trademark taken from the Three Towers on the coat of arms of the city of Copenhagen. The additional words, "First Edition," are found in the 1974 bell. Around the outer base, in lovely script, are lines from Lord Tennyson's *In Memoriam:*

> "Ring out the old,
> Ring in the new,
> Ring out wild bells!"

Every bell is cast in a plaster mold which is destroyed at the end of the year. Bells are carefully put together by hand and retouched to take away the fine lines of the mold.

seems to smile on everyone? For the very reason that it lacks the rugged grandeur of the other Scandinavian countries, does its compactness give it added charm: its patchwork of farmsteads and villages, its stands of beechwood, its humble cottages with thatched roofs, and seagulls making white patterns against the sky? Is it sometimes like a fairyland of sorts, where the artist breathes the charm of native folk into his work—just as their master storyteller, Hans Christian Andersen, wove his melancholy, failures, and his simple joys into a happy song? "Life itself," he often said, "is the most wonderful fairytale of all!"

The delightful naiveté of children, evident in Hans Andersen's tales, is shared by Bing and Grøndahl craftsmen in the simple clarity of form and substance evident in their figurines, plates, and bells. And throughout the world, collectors take these treasures to their hearts, appreciating this revelation too of the Danish temperament with its simple, joyous interpretation of life.

Roskilde Cathedral, honored on Bing and Grøndahl's First Edition Year Bell issued in 1974, has been the burial place for Danish monarchs since 1412. Thirty-seven kings and queens are buried there. The latest, King Frederik IX, was interred in 1971 in the chapel of Christian IX.

The Year Bell, as all other ceramic creations, begins with an unshapely lump of clay. In Denmark, ingredients of porcelain—quartz, kaolin, and feldspar—as well as coloring and firing materials, must be imported. After the first firing, the various parts of the bell are assembled and retouched to take away all traces of the fine lines of the mold.

Decoration in the famous cobalt blue is done by hand: the 1974 bell on a relief of wild mistletoe, and the relief pattern for the 1975 bell being pomegranate with its fruits and flowers.

After painting, the bell is dipped into the glaze vat, and the color immediately disappears under a lusterless, gray-white film. But during the hard-firing which follows, the glaze fuses and becomes transparent like glass, and the colors again appear, beautifully distinct underneath the glaze. This is followed by the 22-karat gold decoration, done by hand. At the end of the year, the mold is destroyed.

"All great works of art look as if they were done in joy," said Robert Henri. And Bing and Grøndahl's Year Bells are the most current evidence that Denmark abounds in joyous creativity. Does this vibrant spontaneity come partly from the Danish countryside that

Decoration in the famous underglaze blue is done by hand, the relief pattern changing from year to year.

The city of Roskilde, the original capital of Denmark and residence of Danish monarchs in Viking days, is located 20 miles from the center of Copenhagen and has a population of 50,000. King Harald Bluetooth built a wooden church near the royal residence there in 960 A.D. Later, Absalon, bishop of Roskilde and founder of Copenhagen, replaced the first structure with today's red brick cathedral. His grandson, Canute the Great, raised its status to that of a bishop's church.

Over the centuries there have been many changes, much adding, much taking away. Royal chapels and porches have been added; numerous towers and spires have been raised. White Gothic vaulting soars up over 80 feet. From east to west the cathedral measures 275 feet, the second longest church in Denmark; the building is 82 feet wide. It is easily Denmark's most significant architecture from the Middle Ages, combining Gothic and Romanesque styles, and representing hundreds of years of Danish architecture. Since there is a similar cathedral in France, historians suspect that the cathedral's unknown architect is either a Frenchman or a Dane who studied in France.

The cathedral organ dates back to 1555. Through the years it has been rebuilt again and again. Its 5000 pipes vary in length from a few centimeters to nine meters. In 1957, over 15,000 hours were spent on its restoration. Experts believe that in its present condition it should last several centuries.

Queen Margrethe I, who died in 1412, was the first monarch to be buried in Roskilde. It was the largest church event in all Scandinavia. Requiems were held at 50 altars simultaneously, and during the following two days a number of added requiem services were held.

The daughter of Valdemar IV, Margrethe was married to King Haakon of Norway. When the king died in 1380, she acted as regent for her infant son, Olaf, until his death in 1387. At that time she was proclaimed queen of both Norway and Denmark, and a year later she was named queen of Sweden too. After helping her people get rid of their repudiated king, Albert of Meklenburg, she convinced the three kingdoms to unite. They were joined in 1397 by the Union of Kalmar, which also preserved the privileges and laws of each country. At this time, Denmark was in a state of ascendency that the nation has not known since. Margrethe's reign proved to be the greatest period of all. She was an astute and subtle diplomat, as shrewd as any king.

After glazing, the bells are decorated in 22-karat gold.

Margrethe died during the plague of 1412. Her alabaster statue, which in some strange way captures her enigmatic beauty, lies on her tomb in Roskilde. One feels she may awaken at any moment. . . . After her death and far into the 19th century, two schoolboys sang every morning at her tomb.

In side chapels and in alabaster tombs behind the high altar, other monarchs lie at rest. Engraved on their monuments or depicted in paintings are scenes from their lives. Flowers are often placed on the tomb of Christian X, the late king's father, who so courageously defied the Nazis in the trying days of the 40s.

Historians tell us that in countless ways Roskilde Cathedral is surely Denmark's greatest church, being through long years to Denmark what Westminster Abbey is to England.

In 1968, the Margrethe Spire was destroyed by fire. It not only burned out the spire, but the twin bells were melted into a heap of molten metal amid the ashes. By a sheer stroke of fortune, the Ministry of Ecclesiastical Affairs had a tape recording of the peal of the old bells. Photographs of the bells were then found, and all of Denmark was caught up in the excitement of restoring the historic bells. Architects set to work collecting all the scraps of the bells they could find. A Danish metal company purified the metal, and under heavy guard it was sent to Holland. Here it was recast into new bells. Here their peal was regulated to the peal on the tape recording. And in 1970, the new bells with the old peal were hoisted into the reconstructed Margrethe Spire.

As the motif for the 1975 Year Bell, Bing and Grøndahl chose *San Pietro in Vaticano, Roma*—St. Peter's in the Vatican State in Rome. It was chosen for this particular year because those who are of the Roman Catholic faith celebrate 1975 as a year of jubilee. This celebration, instituted in Leviticus 25, to be held every 50 years, has since 1300 been held every 25 years by order of Pope Bonifacius. In 1950, the latest year of jubilee, for many Catholics throughout the world all roads did indeed lead to Rome, and there was an enormous influx of pilgrims to the Vatican.

St. Peter's, with its majestic history, is the largest cathedral in the world. Its crowning glory is its magnificent dome which soars over the crossing of the church, directly over what legend says is the Apostle Peter's tomb. It stands on the site of an earlier church built in 324 A.D. Centuries later, this first San Pietro was torn down, after years of patching were of no avail. Building the new church was begun by order of Pope Julius II in 1506.

At that time, Bramante, who was commissioned by the pope to make the first plans, envisioned the church as a Greek cross with a great central dome. Alterations in his plan were made by his successors —Raphael, Peruzzi, and Antonio da Sangello the Younger. No doubt, in combining the ideas of a number of great artists and architects, there are some incongruities aesthetically. But the single quality which every feature of the church has in common is immensity.

Later, when Michelangelo worked on the cathedral, he returned to Bramante's Greek cross form, although he simplified the scheme and redesigned the dome so that it soars 452 feet above the ground. He wanted it to dominate the skyline of Rome as a fitting symbol of Christendom. It does that and more. This notable Renaissance structure, this largest cathedral, dominates the entire landscape, and as you approach it you are lost in its overwhelming magnificence.

It takes 50,000 people to make a crowd in the church, and more than 80,000 can attend at one time. A square, directly in front of the church, connects with the huge oval in the foreground. Light colored stone forms a floor for the huge outdoor room. A fountain on either side and the central obelisk point to the arching sky which provides a ceiling for this noted square.

St. Peter's is filled with treasures that have been collected over the centuries. One column, said to be from the temple in Jerusalem, has unique value to those who believe Christ may have leaned against it. Large mosaic copies of paintings that adorn the interior deceive the most expert, so much do they carry the illusion of an oil painting.

Perhaps the primary beauty of this cathedral is found in its historical context, in the living continuity of Christian worship. But the colossal structure, the monumental statues of the Savior and the apostles, the enormous interior richly furnished in fine colored marble and glorious mosaics do speak to one. Among the most celebrated treasures are Michelangelo's *Pieta* and his *Moses*. "It surpasses all power of description," wrote Mendelssohn about this cathedral. "It appears to me like some great work of nature, a forest, a mass of rocks, or something similar; for I can never realize the idea that it is a work of man."

Cathedral bells! We hear them now at Christmas in a special way. In Scandinavian countries, church bells "chime in Christmas" at five o'clock on Christmas Eve. And bells at the great cathedral of Roskilde ring out too, calling everyone to church before the home festivities begin—goose and rice porridge, tales of *Julenissen,* and circling the tree with locked hands while singing Christmas songs.

In Italy, Christmas is announced at midnight from every belfry. In great cities, in the smallest villages, the people come to pay their homage to the Child. Shepherds wend their way down from the hills playing their pipes. And the great bronze bell from St. Peter's, its tone echoing "across the piazza like a paternal call from distant Jehovah," calls the people to worship.

Listen to the bells! They ring out across the hills and the valleys and the plains. And their message, meant for everyone, does not change:

> *I bring you tidings of great joy. . . .*
> *Unto you is born this day*
> *in the city of David*
> *a Saviour. . . .*

Stamps Tell the Christmas Story

AGNES HARRIGAN MUELLER

CHRISTMAS stamps tell a story. They tell of the wonder and mystery and miracle of the birth of the Child who is God. Through miniature reproductions of paintings of old masters, through contemporary art designed by adults and children, through Christmas themes expressed in stained glass windows, we see interpretations of the annunciation, the manger birth, the heavenly host singing the glad song, the shepherds' visit, and the Wise Men's gifts. Even though the Christ child was born 2000 years ago, the glad tidings are told through stamps today by countries throughout the world. And every version is fresh. Every telling is new!

Stamp collecting is easily the world's most popular hobby. Historians claim that collecting was born when an advertisement appeared in a London newspaper to the effect that a young lady wanted to accumulate enough of the new postage stamps to paper her room. She would be grateful for any sent her. . . .

During the past 10 years, Christmas stamp collecting has increased more than any philatelic specialty. Over 100 countries issued Christmas stamps this year, some providing several designs, some making their use obligatory during December.

Stamp historians give Canada credit for being the first country to issue a Christmas stamp. Designed by Warren T. Green, the stamp had no religious theme but pictured the British Empire in red on a map of the world. It was inscribed "Xmas 1898."

CHRISTMAS ISLAND 1972
"Peace and Joy"
Staff Artist

GREAT BRITAIN 1969
"The Three Shepherds"
Fritz Wegner

CANADA 1965
"Gifts of the Wise Men"
Helen Fitzgerald

UNITED STATES 1974
Detail of angel from
"The Perusis Altarpiece"
Metropolitan Museum of Art

GHANA 1971
Holy season—Ghanese style

NEW ZEALAND 1962
"Madonna in Prayer"
Il Sassoferrato

TRINIDAD and TOBAGO 1970
"Virgin and Child
with St. John and Angel"
Morando

Stamps pictured here are oversized.

ANGUILLA 1970
"Adoration of the Magi"
Giovanni Battista Tiepolo

SPAIN 1960
"Adoration of the Magi"
Detail from painting
"The Holy Family"
Velasquez

BRAZIL 1973
Angel bursts through clouds
to sing hallelujahs
Jayme M. Kopke, Age 13

UNITED STATES 1965
Based on painting by
Lucile Gloria Chabat

WESTERN SAMOA 1970
"Prince of Peace"
Melane Fe'ac

GILBERT and ELLICE ISLANDS 1970
(Child with halo on pandanus mat)
Terry Collis

In 1906, Romania, the second nation to issue a Christmas stamp, pictured the angel Gabriel in the annunciation. Through the years, Gabriel has appeared on the stamps of 41 countries. Vatican City issued three airmail stamps in 1956 featuring Gabriel: a painting by Malozzo do Forli, a mosaic by Cavallina, and a detail from Leonardo da Vinci's "The Annunciation to Mary."

Archangel Gabriel, blowing his horn, was placed as a weathervane on People's Methodist Church at Newburyport, Mass., in 1840. This weathervane is depicted on the United States Christmas stamp for 1965, from a 1939 watercolor by Lucile Gloria Chabat. In 1968, the stamp for our country featured Gabriel in Flemish artist Jan Van Eyck's painting, "The Annunciation." Brazil's stamp in 1971 is a miniature showing Gabriel in a stained glass window, in the upper choir of the Franciscan Convent at Rio de Janeiro.

Frequently, Christmas stamps depict Mary and the Christ child or Mary alone. In its Christmas series, New Zealand reproduced a number of masterpieces of art. In 1962, they used "Madonna in Prayer" by Il Sassoferrato, a 17th century Italian artist, who pictured the Virgin Mary in an attitude of prayer—her hands clasped, her eyes downcast. The painting now hangs in Vatican Pinacotece, Rome. In 1972, one of the stamps issued by the United States was a detail from "Mary, Queen of Heaven," by an artist of the 16th century identified only as "The Master of the St. Lucy Legend." It is in the Samuel H. Kress collection in the National Gallery of Art, Washington, D.C. Ethiopia, Costa Rica, and Australia pictured the Madonna and Child on their 1962 issues.

Hungary printed a set of three stamps in 1943. One pictured an angel announcing the Savior's birth to shepherds as they knelt in awe; in the second, the shepherds worshipped at the crib of Jesus; and the third depicted the visit of the Wise Men.

The adoration of the magi is another frequently used subject. Spain issued a stamp in 1960 which reproduced the painting, "Adoration of the Kings," by the Spanish artist Velasquez who pictured the Wise Men in clothes typical of the era in which the artist lived. In 1961, New Zealand's stamp was a reproduction of a painting by German artist Albrecht Dürer, picturing the magi presenting gifts to the Christ child.

In 1973, Monaco honored St. Francis of Assisi who is credited with erecting the first crèche 750 years ago. Six stamps were issued there depicting the crèche as painted by famous artists of the 14th and 15th centuries.

In 1972 Australia's stamp portrayed the baptism of Christ with the title, "This is my beloved Son." The same year, their Christmas airmail stamp depicted the text, John 10:14—"I am the good shepherd." Both stamps were designed by George Hamori, in the style of 15th century woodcuts.

The first Christmas stamp issued in the United States, in 1962, was designed to include traditional holiday symbols—lighted tapers and an evergreen wreath tied with red ribbon. The second stamp went on sale at Santa Claus, Ind., in November, 1963, reproducing a three-color painting of the National Christmas Tree located near the White House. At that time, Christmas stamps were issued in sheets of 100.

The first United States four-in-one issue was printed in 1964. Traditional symbols—a poinsettia, a branch of mistletoe, a sprig of holly, and a pine twig with a cone—were printed in red and green against a white background. In 1966, when our Christmas stamp pictured the Madonna and Child from a painting by 15th century Flemish painter Hans Memling, (followed by an enlarged version of this stamp for 1967), selling stamps of a religious nature created a national controversy. A group of Protestants and Other Americans for Separation of Church and State sued the Postmaster General. They charged that the use of religious imagery on stamps is prohibited by the First Amendment.

The controversy was finally resolved in 1970 when the Court of Appeals ruled that it was no more objectionable to show a religious painting on a postage stamp than to show the painting in a government museum. Subsequently, the Post Office Department decided to offer one religious and one secular stamp each year.

In 1971, the United States religious stamp was a reproduction of a detail of the 16th century painting, "Adoration of the Shepherds," from the Samuel H. Kress collection in the National Gallery of Art, Washington, D.C. The secular stamp pictured "A Partridge in a Pear Tree" painted by Jamie Wyeth of Chadds Ford, Pa.

Steven Dohanos, a Westport, Conn., artist who served as chairman of the Citizens' Stamp Advisory Committee in 1973, recommended that the secular stamp for that year picture a Christmas tree stitched in needlepoint by Dolli Tingle. The religious stamp was a reproduction of the Madonna and Child painted by Raphael around 1505.

Children as well as adults have designed admirable Christmas stamps. In 1970, Canadian educators asked

MONACO 1973
Nativity Crèche
From the Flemish school

UNITED STATES 1974
"The Road—Winter"
Currier and Ives

AUSTRIA 1954
"Child and Christmas Tree"
Staff artist

CUBA 1956
The Three Wise Men

UNITED STATES 1973
"Madonna and Child"
Raphael
Cowper Collection
National Gallery of Art
Washington, D.C.

UNITED STATES 1964
Holly—Mistletoe—Wintamen
Poinsettia—Fenton
Pine cone—Bower
Overall design—Naegele

CANADA 1970
"Horse-drawn Sleigh" Donna Niskala, 9
"Snowman and Christmas Tree" Manon LeCompte, 9
"Santa Claus" Eugene Bhattacharya, 7
"Christ Child" Janet McKinney, 8

UNITED STATES 1974
Dove of Peace
Weathervane from Mount Vernon

AUSTRALIA 1969
"Nativity"
George Hamori

COSTA RICA 1969
"Madonna and Child"
Staff Artist

UNITED STATES 1966
"Madonna and Child with Angels"
Hans Memling
National Gallery of Art
Washington, D.C.

ROMANIA 1906
Archangel Gabriel

school children under 12 to design a stamp on the theme "What Christmas Means to Me." Of the 50,000 designs submitted, 12 were selected to be used as Canadian Christmas stamps that year. In 1973, Brazil issued a million copies of a stamp—designed by 13-year-old Jayme M. Kopke—showing an angel bursting through clouds to sing joyful hallelujahs.

Some years ago, a common interest in collecting religious stamps, and learning the stories behind them, led several hundred philatelists in the United States to form an organization called COROS—Collectors of Religion on Stamps. They publish a bimonthly magazine, the *COROS CHRONICLE*. In 1972, the editor of the magazine, Waller A. Sager, in collaboration with Kathleen M. Berry, editor of *The Fine Arts Philatelist*, published a handbook entitled *Seventy-Five Years of Christmas Stamps.*

A smaller group of philatelists formed the Protestant Study Group of COROS to do more intensive research on Protestant people and associated places on stamps. They publish the quarterly journal *Protestant Philately*.

In 1969, plans were initiated to organize the Christmas Philatelic Club. These plans were carried out, and by 1974 the membership had grown to nearly 500. Most members live in the United States, but Canada, England, Germany, New Zealand, the Netherlands, and Puerto Rico claim a share of them too. Virginia Haywood, publisher of their journal, *Yule Log*, generously offered stamps from her collection which are used as illustrations for this article. Members of the club say that as they collect Christmas stamps and read monthly issues of their journal, they celebrate the festival of Christmas in a special way month by month the year round.

In the United States alone, Christmas stamp collecting has become such a philatelic favorite that during the last three years two billion Christmas stamps were issued each year. Each of these bits of paper, along with stamps issued by many other countries, tells its own story: the prophecy of Jesus' birth, the angel Gabriel's message, the Magnificat, Caesar's decree, the birth in the manger, the shepherds' visit, the angels' song, gifts of the Wise Men, the flight into Egypt. All are fragments that make up the wonder and mystery and miracle of the birth of the Child who is God.

Today, through Christmas stamps, the world is confronted in a new way by the old, ever-new story of the manger Child. And the humble, commercial postage stamp becomes a mighty force as it, too, goes on its way, bearing the great, glad tidings.

Majestic Gift

Marion Olmon Lien   Robert Wetzler

1. Ma - jes - tic gift now giv'n in in - fant form to hold the
2. Ma - jes - tic gift! The whole of God's re-demp - tive plan be-
3. Ma - jes - tic gift! What love from God the Fa - ther's throne can
4. An - gel - ic voic-es shout ec - stat - ic, wild ac - claim un-

long a - wait-ed hope of man by proph-et's writ fore - told; for
fore all worlds and through all time to be now comes to man. Leap
give his Son that tru - ly I might claim him as my own? A
til all heav'n re - sounds with joy. All glo - ry to his name! In

us the Son is born! The Christ, the liv - ing Word, Re-
up, my wait - ing soul, on soar-ing wings take flight. To
path-way clear - ly laid; from earth to heav'n its span; the
an - ti - phon now sing the hearts of men on earth. The

deem - er, Heal - er, Prince of Peace, blest Mas - ter, Sav - ior, Lord.
men who long in dark - ness walked is come e - ter - nal light.
glo - ry of al - might - y God made vis - i - ble to man.
King! The King is come em - bod - ied in this ho - ly birth!

This Night There Comes to Bethlehem

Een kint gheboren in Bethlehem
Tr., Beatrice Quickenden

15th century Dutch
Arr., David S. Walker

1. This night there comes to Beth - le-hem a child, then sing Je-ru - sa-lem, A - mor, a - mor, a - mor, a - mor, a - mor, quam dul-cis est a-mor!*

2. A man-ger holds this lit - tle one, al - might-y God's be - lov - ed Son. A-mor, a - mor, a - mor, a - mor, a - mor, quam dul-cis est a-mor! 3. "Let

* O love, O love,...what sweetness is his love!

peace be o - ver all the earth," an an - gel cries at this sweet birth. A -

mor, a - mor, a - mor, a - mor, a - mor, quam dul - cis est a - mor!

All Poor Men and Humble

Free trans. from the Welsh, K.E. Roberts

Gordon H. Carlson

1. All poor men and
2. Though Wise Men who
3. Then haste we to

1. hum - ble, all lame men who stum - ble, come with
2. found him laid rich gifts a - round him, yet ox - en
3. show him the prais - es we owe him, our ser - vice

haste and feel not a-fraid; for Je -
they gave him their hay: and Je -
he ne'er can de-spise: whose love

sus, our trea-sure, with love past all mea-sure,
sus in beau-ty ac-cept-ed their du-ty;
still is a-ble to show us that sta-ble

in low-ly poor man-ger was laid.
con-tent-ed in man-ger he lay.
where soft-ly in man-ger he lies.

poco rit. ppp

Look Where All the Starlight Glows

Herbert Brokering

Edward Lewis
Arr., Ronald A. Nelson

1. Look where all the star-light glows; _____ kneel be-side the swad-dling clothes; _____ feel the way _____ the east wind blows; _____ see how swift the shep-herd goes. _____
2. Stop and lis-ten where you are; _____ find him near when he _____ seems far; _____ watch the glow _____ of dis-tant star; _____ find the Je - sus where you are. _____
3. Ring the bells and watch the sky; _____ come, O Je - sus, do _____ come by; _____ hear our laugh _____ and see us cry; _____ tell us when and tell us why. _____

Tiny Baby, Holy Baby

John H. Payne

Alphonsus Liguori, 1696-1787
Arr., David N. Johnson

1. The
2. There

1. night was clear and cold when the Son of God was
2. was no room for him at the inn that win - ter

1. born;____ his moth - er held him close to her
2. day.____ A man - ger was his cra - dle that

1. heart to keep him warm. Ti - ny ba - by, ho - ly
2. held him as he lay. Ti - ny ba - by, ho - ly

Morning Star, O Cheering Sight

Johann Scheffler, 1624 - 1677
Tr., Bennet Harvey, Jr., 1829 - 1894

Hagen
F. F. Hagen, 1818 - 1907

SOLO

1. Morn-ing Star, O cheer-ing sight! Ere Thou cam'st how dark earth's night!
2. Morn-ing Star, thy glo-ry bright far ex-cels the sun's clear light:
3. Thy glad beams, thou Morn-ing Star, cheer the na-tions near and far.
4. Morn-ing Star, my soul's true light, tar-ry not, dis-pel my night;

CHORUS

Morn-ing Star, O cheer-ing sight! Ere Thou cam'st how dark earth's night!
Morn-ing Star, thy glo-ry bright far ex-cels the sun's clear light.
Thy glad beams, thou Morn-ing Star, cheer the na-tions near and far;
Morn-ing Star, my soul's true light, tar-ry not, dis-pel my night;

SOLO — CHORUS — SOLO — CHORUS

Je-sus mine, in me shine; in me shine, Je-sus mine;
Je-sus be, con-stant-ly, con-stant-ly, Je-sus be
thee we own, Lord a-lone, Lord a-lone, thee we own,
Je-sus mine, in me shine; in me shine, Je-sus mine;

fill my heart with light di-vine.
more than thou-sand suns to me.
man's great Sav-ior, God's dear Son.
fill my heart with light di-vine. A-men.

From *Hymnal of the Moravian Church.*

A Moravian Christmas

KARL KROEGER

Members of the Old Salem Chorus perform Christmas anthems.

CHRISTMAS is always celebration. And in the Moravian tradition, part of the celebration is the Christmas Eve Lovefeast—sharing the simple fare of a brown bun and steaming coffee. But to Moravians, it is a symbolic sharing of food and drink as an act of fellowship, and in a singular way it is a rich and fulfilling feast of the heart.

This Christmas custom was included almost from the beginning when the Moravians, a small band of German immigrants, came to America in 1735 to evangelize among the American Indians. Their first efforts in Georgia had been unsuccessful, and in 1740 they abandoned that colony for more promising opportunities among the Delawares in Pennsylvania. They laid the foundations of their first congregational community to serve as a base of operations for the missionary work.

Now, quite unexpectedly, Count Nicholas Ludwig von Zinzendorf, the man primarily responsible for molding their various ideas into a cohesive direction, arrived just in time to celebrate Christmas, 1741, with them. They ushered in Christmas Day with the observance on Christmas Eve of the Vigils of Christmas, which includes the lovefeast celebrated in the midst of joyful Christmas sounds from bells, horns, pipes, and happy voices. It was celebration, indeed.

Part of the log house in which the congregation was meeting also housed the community animals.

Zinzendorf, sensing an opportunity to impress the significance of Christ's birth more deeply in the minds of the congregation, led them to the part of the house where the animals were kept. There he began to sing an old German Epiphany hymn by Adam Drese, *"Jesu rufe mich"* (Jesus Call Thou Me). One of the verses of the hymn went as follows:

> Not Jerusalem,
> Rather Bethlehem
>   Gave us that which
>   Maketh life rich;
> Not Jerusalem.

The community had not yet been named, and the verse of that hymn suggested one—Bethlehem. Thus a hymn may be considered responsible for the naming of the first Moravian congregational town in America, on Christmas Eve, 1741.

The Moravian Church traces its origins back to the followers of John Hus, the 15th-century Czech religious reformer who was martyred for his beliefs in 1415. In 1457 his followers founded a society called the *Unitas Fratrum* (the Unity of Brethren). Ten years later they broke with the Roman Catholic Church, forming what is considered to be the oldest Protestant denomination. The society thrived in Bohemia, Moravia, and Poland until the height of the Counter-Reformation, when efforts were made to

61

suppress it along with other Protestant groups. This oppression resulted in the Thirty Years War (1618-1648), during which the *Unitas Fratrum* was scattered and suppressed. Faith and traditions were kept alive secretly, passed on from parent to child, until in 1722 a small group of refugees from Moravia settled on the estate of Count Nicholas Ludwig von Zinzendorf in Saxony. Zinzendorf, a pious nobleman with an evangelical bent, offered them protection and encouraged the renewal of their church. Many of the customs, particularly the musical customs of the present-day Moravian Church, date from its renewal in 1722 and the years following.

In the year following the first Christmas in Bethlehem, many improvements were made in the village. New houses were built, a community government was organized, and in June 1742 the size of the town was more than doubled by the arrival of 56 persons from Europe. Zinzendorf was still among them, pursuing his dream of organizing the various Christian churches in Pennsylvania into an interdenominational society for Christ—a plan that had little hope of success among the rival factions of that time.

On December 24, 1742, the Christmas Eve Vigils were again held. The community diary describes the scene as follows:

The Bethlehem Christmas Hymn

Count Zinzendorf   1742   FIDEL UNITAS
Traditional melody

Hymn 254 in *Hymnal of the Moravian Church.*

"The congregation assembled at 11 o'clock for the *Christmas Eve Vigil,* to observe it in fellowship with our German congregations in Europe. [It should be noted that the "official" date in Pennsylvania was December 13, since Great Britain still used the Old Style calendar. The fact that the Moravians observed the New Style date for Christmas caused them some difficulty with certain of their neighbors, since it was used as evidence that they were secretly Papists.] It opened with a lovefeast. Mention was made of the fact that today just a year ago Bethlehem received its name. . . .

"On this festive occasion Bro. Ludwig [Zinzendorf] sang the impromptu hymn *O blessed night, without compare on earth, The night whereon the Wonder-Child had birth!* We spent these blessed hours of Christmas Eve in adoring contemplation of this Son of God and man in his lowly birth and continued in adoring meditation and veneration until 1 o'clock in the morning."

Zinzendorf had a gift for composing extemporaneous and impromptu hymns. He had done it many times in

Germany, so that his performance on this occasion was not unexpected. It is, however, the earliest Moravian hymn known to have been written in America. It contains 37 stanzas, covers Christ's earthly journey from birth to resurrection, with allusions to the contemporary situation. The hymn is still used in part today in the Christmas Eve Vigils observed in Bethlehem, Pa.

Christmas has always ranked high in the festivals of the Moravian Church, second only to Holy Week and Easter in importance. Over the years the church has developed certain traditions and customs connected with Christmas that are unique to it, or that have passed from it into wider use in the Christian church. One of these customs, the Christmas Eve Lovefeast, a modern revival of the Christian *Agape,* was revived in the Moravian Church in 1727 by Count Zinzendorf. Lovefeasts are held many times during the year to celebrate church festivals, to honor important visitors, to commemorate memorable occasions. During the 18th century it was not uncommon

The Moravian Star brightens homes and churches during Christmas.

for a congregation to hold as many as eight to ten lovefeasts each month.

For the Christmas Eve Lovefeast several traditions have been handed down that are unique. The first of these is the distribution of lighted candles to the congregation. This practice dates from 1747 in Marienborn, Germany. At first it was limited only to the children of the congregation who celebrated a lovefeast several hours before the Christmas Eve Vigils. Later the children's service in many places was combined with the adult celebration, and all were given candles.

The candles are, of course, symbolic. They are to remind every person of Christ's words: "I am the light of the world," and "Ye are the light of the world. . . . Let your light shine before men, that they may see your good works and give glory to your Father who is in heaven." As they sing an appropriate verse of a hymn toward the end of the service, the candles are held aloft in the darkened church, creating a richly spiritual and deeply moving experience.

Another tradition in the Moravian Church is the *Putz*, a diorama of the Nativity, placed in a public place. Just when the *Putz* was first used in the Moravian Church in America is unknown, but as early as the mid-18th century, school children would scour the forests for moss and evergreens to use to decorate the scene. Some of the scenes included the manger, the adoration of the shepherds, and the coming of the magi. Many Moravian families also have a family Putz, passing on the figures from generation to generation as prized heirlooms. The purpose is simply to reinforce the telling of the story of the first Christmas.

The most recent Christmas custom to achieve the rank of tradition is the Moravian Star. This is a large, multipointed, three-dimensional lighted star which had its origins in Niesky, Germany about 1850. In most churches it is hung prominently before the congregation and is lighted on the first Sunday in Advent to burn through Epiphany. Many Moravian homes also include the star in their Christmas decorations, either outside the house or inside with the Christmas tree and other decorations.

Music plays an important role in all Moravian services, but is particularly important in the Christmas Eve Lovefeast. During the 18th and 19th centuries, composers, most of whom were also Moravian ministers, wrote anthems, songs, and hymns for the Moravian Church services. Most of this music is still preserved today, and is considered to be the finest, most sophisticated music written in America at the time. Many of these songs and anthems were written for the Christmas celebrations.

The earliest Moravian composer to write music in America was Jeremiah Dencke who lived in Bethlehem, Pa., from 1761 to 1795. One of his earliest works is a group of songs and duets written for the Christmas Eve service in Bethlehem in 1767.

John Frederik Peter, another fine musician, arrived in America in 1770 as a young man of 24, after completing work at the seminary. Peter was an organist and violinist, but had no thought of becoming a composer. He soon found that the American Moravian communities needed more music than their modest libraries could provide. He tried his hand at composing music for special services, which was well received by the congregations. Peter served as music

The Salem Band plays Christmas chorales in Old Salem, North Carolina.

director and composer in many American Moravian communities: Bethlehem, Nazareth, and Lititz in Pennsylvania; Salem in North Carolina; Graceham in Maryland; and Hope in New Jersey. Among his sacred songs and anthems, his Christmas anthem, "Sing, O Ye Heavens," written in the early 1800s, has long been a favorite in the Moravian Church.

John Antes, one of the most gifted Moravian composers, was born in Pennsylvania in 1740. He was sent as a missionary to Egypt in 1770, and later lived in England from 1786 until his death in 1811. He was one of the most gifted of the Moravian composers. His vocal solo, "Loveliest Immanuel," and a Christmas anthem, "Shout Ye Heavens," written during the 1790s, are two of the most moving and sophisticated compositions by an American composer of the 18th century.

Many other musicians contributed to the music for the Moravian Christmas celebration. Some of the chorales date back to the old *Unitas Fratrum*. Some composers were not members of the Moravian Church, for example, J. A. P. Schulz, whose anthem, "Thou Child Divine," was very popular with Moravians at Christmas. In more recent times traditional Christmas carols such as "O Come, All Ye Faithful," "Silent Night," and "Hark, the Herald Angels Sing," are included along with traditional Moravian hymns and chorales, giving the lovefeast a more popular and even an ecumenical flavor.

The Moravian Christmas piece that has achieved the most popularity over the years is Francis F. Hagen's "Morning Star, O Cheering Sight." The work was composed about 1836 while Hagen was a teacher at the boys' school in Salem, N.C. It was published in 1857 and again in 1890, and made its way into the Christmas services of many denominations. Hagen was one of the last of the "classical" Moravian composers. He, like many of his predecessors, was an active minister, serving congregations in North Carolina, Pennsylvania, New York, and Iowa. He was a powerful preacher, a writer of some distinction, and a musician of remarkable ability. Many of his anthems are quite advanced harmonically for their time. But of all his compositions, the simple and uncomplicated "Morning Star, O Cheering Sight" remains his best known and best-loved composition.

A Moravian Christmas requires the full use of all the senses—sight, hearing, taste, touch, and smell—to receive the full measure of the experience. Preparations begin a month to six weeks or more in advance, with the making of beeswax candles, gathering moss for the *Putz*, making Moravian cookies, and other Christmas projects. A sense of anticipation gradually builds that culminates in the transcending beauty of the Christmas Eve Lovefeast.

This Christmas the 156 Moravian churches in the United States and Canada will join with other Moravian churches throughout the world to celebrate the birth of Christ in much the way their forebears did over two centuries ago. Some things have changed, of course. But the spiritual essence of the Moravian Christmas celebration is the same: beautiful in simplicity and sincerity, joyous in reverence and good will.

The Christmas Eve Lovefeast and Candle Service at Home Moravian Church, Winston-Salem, N.C.

A Christmas Tree Story

GEORGE H. STRALEY

Illustrated by Melva Mickelson

There is a place around the corner where Christmas trees are offered for sale. They are splendid trees, propped in a row against the bare brick wall of a vacant warehouse, under a string of bare electric bulbs. They make a fragrant spot of greenery in a drab neighborhood.

An old man tends these wares . . . an old man with sparkling blue eyes, a drooping white moustache, and a nose the color of a hollyberry. He is stooped and gnome-like, but there is a look of strength about him. He wears a long patched coat and faded scarf, a hat that has lost its brim, and mended mittens. He smokes a cob pipe, and on cold days he slaps his mittens together and stamps his feet.

"Trees!" he cries. "Nice trees! Who'll buy a tree for Christmas?" His voice is not loud but surprisingly resonant.

He was born somewhere in the Old Country, but it would be difficult to say exactly where. Wherever it was, you have a feeling that it was a land of fir trees . . . a region of spruce and balsam like the Pyrenees, the Hochwald, or the Carpathians . . . and that he grew up among them.

He is always at this place along the warehouse wall. He was there last year and he will be there next year. Where he is from one Yuletide to another, no one seems to know.

This old man, when business is slow, will tell you a story. He will not press it on you; you must pry it from him. You must stop and look at his trees when no one else is around. You must admire the trees, but you must appear to be undecided. You must look about you uncertainly and with just the right mixture of interest and abstraction. Finally you must engage him in conversation, and when those keen blue eyes have appraised you and approved you, the mittened hand may withdraw the cob pipe from under the drooping white moustache, and he may say something like this:

"You have heard legends of the Christmas tree, perhaps, have you not? There are many. More legends than trees, almost. Let me tell you the one I like best —an old story from the Old Country, old before my father's grandfather was born." His face cracks into a grin and the blue eyes twinkle. "When I have finished, maybe you decide to buy a tree, eh? . . . Well, then, it is this way . . .

"Once upon a time, as the old storybooks used to say, there was a rich and powerful nobleman who held dominion over a vast estate. It was in the days of feudalism, you understand, when there were lords and overlords, and vassals and peasants. That is to say, it was a very long time ago, though there are lords and overlords and vassals and peasants in the Old Country today too. Not quite in the same fashion, of course, but always there are the ruling classes and the serving classes, are there not?

"This nobleman was a harsh and tyrannical person, with very little of human kindness in him. In name only was he a Christian, though he was by no means eccentric on that account, for there are many such in the world. Don't you agree? But he was also a sly and clever man of great ambitions, and exceedingly anxious to stand high in the favor of the king, so that whatever decree the king issued he was most prompt and faithful to carry out.

65

"Now the king was a ruler of considerable piety for those times. The country had passed through much quarrelsomeness and strife, and this was a period of what the historians call interregnum; an era of comparative tranquility, you understand, with old passions put at rest and new values being searched for by the more thoughtful among men.

"So it was that when the Yuletide season came round the king proclaimed an edict that there should be decent and suitable festivities in all the great manor houses, and that all his subjects, whatever their class or condition, should bestow a gift to the seigniors of their respective estates. Each man was to give according to his circumstances, and the bounties were then to be divided up by the overlords and parceled out to the poor and needy.

"It was a virtuous design, wouldn't you say, sir? And for my part I have always thought that the king was well ahead of his time. But in any case, there was this particular nobleman, seignior of an estate, eager to do the king's bidding but crafty for his own aims, as all such intermediaries are apt to be. He saw that it would be to his best interests to make a fine showing for the royal charity. He saw, also, that if the gifts borne to his manor house were sufficiently generous, there would be enough for him to add to his own personal treasure chests without fear of discovery.

"Ah, he was a selfish rascal—though no more so, perhaps, than many another, then and now. You understand my meaning, sir?

"Well, this nobleman, then—this seignior—made bold to alter the king's decree to this extent: that all husbandmen and vassals and such as held manorial lands in fief should give to the utmost, under pain of punishment. And whereas the king had prescribed that each should give according to his means, this overlord let it be known that only *handsome* bounties would be acceptable, and that any paltry offerings would be a direct affront to the king, meriting appropriate reprisal.

"You may well imagine, sir, that the zeal of this petty tyrant was not in vain. Upon the eve of the Yuletide there was a great celebration in the big reception hall of the manor, as there were in all estates of the realm that night.

"The gifts poured in. Whole families arrived, bearing baskets filled with the choicest products of field and vine, furs and leathers and woven goods, articles of precious metal, little chamois bags of gold coins, and even long-treasured heirlooms, which it was plain to see many parted with reluctantly. The seignior received them all graciously, with a quick eye to their value, and heaped everything together in a great pile in the center of the floor. Then musicians were called in, and preparations were made for dancing and jollity.

"But just as the festivities were about to begin, a poor vassal, half frozen, presented himself at the door. Because his hands were empty the nobleman seized him in anger.

"'Where is your bounty?' he demanded. 'How dare you come here without a suitable gift for the king's charity?'

"'My gift is outside your door,' the miserable fellow made answer. 'I have nothing of value to bring—except this.' And therewith he pointed out to the seignior a great spruce tree, beautifully proportioned, lying in the snow. Beside the tree stood the vassal's brave wife and their three young children, in shabby garments.

"While the nobleman stared at this strange spectacle, fending for words to vent his fury, the vassal said: 'Master, I know that in making this offering I give the king only what is his. But I have loved this tree. I have cared for it. I have felled it with my own hands, and my family and I have dragged it here, tenderly, so as not to break its beautiful branches. I have nothing else to give, and I pray you to accept it as a symbol of my devotion.'

"Then the seignior found his voice. 'Shame upon you! Your gift is a mockery and an insult. You shall be punished for your insolence. Begone, at once!'

"And so saying, he slammed the door upon the unfortunate man.

"For a little while the wretch and his family stood around the felled tree, dazed and frightened, staring strickenly at the lighted windows of the manor house and hearing, as from a long way off, the strains of music within.

"And that, sir, is where the king found them. For the king was abroad that night. He arrived in a gilded sleigh drawn by four black horses, with suitable equipage and outriders. The vassal and his family fell upon their knees in the snow, but the king bade them rise and explain their situation.

"So the poor man told his story as he had told it to the nobleman, and after the king had heard him gravely he said in a kind voice: 'I am disposed to regard that you are a subject of courage and good will, and none such deserves the king's displeasure. Moreover, I perceive that you have a sentimental heart and perhaps a finer fancy than most of those who stand over you. Tell me, what religious symbolism do you see in your tree?'

" 'Sire,' replied the vassal, 'it has seemed to me that the tall and stately firs that grow in this land hold within their branches the very spirit of Christ's Mass. They grow tall and straight, like righteous men. They are forever green, like our Lord's promise of eternal life. When I look upon them, I see them as living spires of the living Church.'

" 'Well spoken,' said the king . . . and to one of his retinue: 'Open the door.'

"Then the door was opened wide, the music and the dancing stopped, and the outraged nobleman, rushing across the hall to discover the meaning of this intrusion, was met by the king's men, carrying the great spruce tree between them. Behind them came the vassal and his family, and behind them strode the king.

" 'Your majesty . . . welcome, your majesty!' stammered the cringing seignior, on his knees. But the king ignored him, and with a gesture indicated that the tree should be placed in the center of the hall. When it had been raised and secured so that it stood majestically erect, he said:

" 'Because this tree is of more worth than all the other gifts, let it tower above them, and let them be displayed on its branches and around its base. And henceforth, this shall be the symbol of Christmas.' "

. . . There is a place around the corner where Christmas trees are offered for sale.

And there is an old man from the Old Country, with sparkling blue eyes, a drooping white moustache, and a nose the color of a hollyberry.

"Trees!" he cries. "Nice trees! Who'll buy a tree for Christmas?"

He was there last year, and he will be back again next year. And if you ask him, he will tell you this story.

Volume I - 1931

Volume II - 1932

Volume III - 1933

Volume IV - 1934

Volume V - 1935

Volume VI - 1936

Volume VII - 1937

Volume VIII - 1938

Volume IX - 1939

Volume X - 1940

Volume XI - 1941

Volume XII - 1942

Volume XIII - 1943

Volume XIV - 1944

Volume XV - 1945

Christmas for 1975...

The 45th volume of *Christmas,* edited since its inception by Randolph E. Haugan, honors again the birth of Jesus through music, words, and art. But it recognizes, too, the significant milestone of our country's bicentennial—our early beginnings and God's help through the years. The type is set in Linotype Caledonia and the headings in Monotype Goudy Blackletter with Lombardic initials. The printing process is photo-offset lithography. *Christma*s is published by Augsburg Publishing House, Minneapolis, Minnesota.

Volume XVI - 1946

Volume XVII - 1947

Volume XVIII - 1948

Volume XIX - 1949

Volume XX - 1950

Volume XXI - 1951

Volume XXII - 1952

Volume XXIII - 1953

Volume XXIV - 1954

Volume XXV - 1955

Volume XXVI -1956

Volume XXVII - 1957

Volume XXVIII - 1958

Volume XXIX - 1959

Volume XXX - 1960

Volume XXXI - 1961

Volume XXXII - 1962

Volume XXXIII - 1963

Volume XXXIV - 1964

Volume XXXV - 1965

Volume XXXVI - 1966

Volume XXXVII - 1967

Volume XXXVIII - 1968

Volume XXXIX - 1969

Volume XL - 1970

Volume XLI - 1971

Volume XLII - 1972

Volume XLIII - 1973

Volume XLIV - 1974